Opportunity

Seize the day. Win at life.

ROB MOORE

First published in Great Britain by John Murray Learning in 2021
An imprint of John Murray Press
A division of Hodder & Stoughton Ltd,
An Hachette UK company

3

Copyright © Rob Moore 2021

A CIP catalogue record for this title is available from the British Library

Trade Paperback ISBN 978 1 473 68554 3
eBook ISBN 978 1 473 68551 2

Typeset by KnowledgeWorks Global Ltd

Printed and bound in Great Britain by Clays Ltd, Elcograf S.p.A.

John Murray Press policy is to use papers that are natural, renewable and recyclable products and made from wood grown in sustainable forests. The logging and manufacturing processes are expected to conform to the environmental regulations of the country of origin.

John Murray Press
Carmelite House
50 Victoria Embankment
London EC4Y 0DZ

www.johnmurraypress.co.uk

Contents

Preface

My dad has always been my hero. Growing up, I looked up to him, especially when it came to entrepreneurship, sports and being a strong person. I've never met anyone who can turn around a business quite like my dad could. He could take a derelict building and turn it into a hotel. He could take the most run-down pub and turn it into a thriving restaurant. He could hustle before social media even knew what the word meant.

He would go to auctions and liquidation sales and buy cheap stock for pennies in the pound for his leisure businesses. He'd negotiate hard. It was a game to him. He'd always pay in cash with the big brown £10 notes folded in half, all the Queen's heads facing the same way, and always in his right-hand back pocket. My eyes would pop out of their sockets whenever he pulled out his big wad of notes.

It seemed that nothing embarrassed him. Whatever he wanted, he'd ask for it – and he'd usually get it. He loves to tell me how he punched way above his weight in marrying my mum, nearly 12 years his junior.

Later, when his bipolar disorder got worse, he never lost his charm and persuasive character. When he was locked away in the high-security ward 5 of Peterborough Hospital – where you need special keys to get through at least four separate doors – he would call my employees and persuade them to come through the first door, then persuade the receptionist to let them through the second and third doors. Then he'd get the nurses to let him out of the fourth door, and out he'd walk with a cigarette hanging off his bottom lip and his trousers hoisted up under his armpits.

He once persuaded one of my employees that he needed a ladder for a 'project' he was doing in hospital. He got them to bring it in through all the security doors (an extendable ladder!) and then he used it to climb over the 12-foot-perimeter fence. He revelled in the delight of attaining his freedom and loved to tell you just how cunning he'd been.

At the height of his illness, he once got himself arrested for stealing thousands of pounds' worth of DIY equipment from Homebase. He loaded up a pallet trolley with an Outback barbeque, gas heater and the largest items he could find, and walked right out of the store in broad daylight. Once out and around the corner, he turned back, pulled up his trousers and told the security guard 'I've just nicked a grands' worth of stock and you are shit at your job.' He seemed to have a great sense of pride about the whole thing, as he V-signed the store security office from the back of the police van.

When my dad is on his emotional highs, he can talk himself into any business building, past any gatekeeper, and in front of any business owner or multimillionaire. He'd pitch crazy, ridiculous inventions and get people to believe in them.

He's raised money for hotels, pubs, cars, horses, bets, properties, crazy inventions drawn like my 5-year-old daughter might, even my school fees as a kid growing up; you name it, he's begged for it, borrowed it and, most often, outright blagged it. He's never had any money to start any of his new ventures, so he's always created everything from nothing, forging opportunities out of nowhere.

He rarely shielded me from any of his ventures or misdemeanours. He took me with him on whatever crazy journey he could, letting me see the ebbs and flows, highs and lows. He moved us around East Anglia and Cambridgeshire many times as he took new opportunities and repeatedly started a new life. I lived in pubs and hotels and big houses and small flats. We all knew as a family that, if things got hard, Dad would get us out of trouble, and we all subscribed to a crazy, exciting lifestyle.

He's head-butted and broken a policeman's nose for having a go at Ian Botham. He's blown up a man's car for sleeping with his first wife while he was stationed abroad with the RAF. He's scared stupid an endless string of boys and men who've gone within 15 miles of my sister. At 60 years old, he was still getting into fights in the pubs he was taking over and renovating. Everyone was equally scared and full of respect for my dad; they loved him as much as they feared him. No one more so than me.

When he was growing up, my dad had a hard life. He was raised in Huddersfield, a northern English town, in relative poverty. His mum died when he was two. His dad never showed any affection towards him, and remarried just so someone could raise his kids, because he couldn't cope alone. He died when my dad was 18. Dad also lost his sister, a mother figure to him, which I think hit him really hard.

Because of this hard upbringing, Dad didn't find it hard to take chances, forge opportunities and make things happen. After all, when you've experienced what he has, what's the worst that can happen when you try for or ask for something?

My dad has made and lost millions over the years. He's had successful pubs, hotels, bars and restaurants, and he's owned lots of real estate. A lot of my dad's customers in the early years were American servicemen on the local US base, and he made some really good friends. Then the Gulf War happened and the US bases in the UK emptied almost overnight – and my dad's hotels, pubs and friends followed suit.

He lost everything, but he managed to scrape together enough money to start a small restaurant, which he turned around from a dump into a thriving carvery restaurant. This time it was two years' worth of roadworks that killed his trade, and once again he scraped the money together for a very run-down pub in Peter-borough, called the Royal Arms. He rolled up his sleeves, cracked his knuckles, bought a massive long-haired Alsatian called Bruno and banned every single person from that pub within the space of a few weeks. I saw him break pool cues by hitting people with them, rugby-tackle drunks, and punch, kick and head-butt people. Bear in mind my dad was nearly 60 at this point, it was him and the dog against a pub full of reprobates.

Within a few months he had established a new carvery restaurant and thriving trade. It had become a family business, and my dad was proud that we were all working together. He ran the pub and carved the meat, my mum was the chef, cooking for more than a hundred people a day, my sister ran the restaurant, and I ran the bar. It all looked rosy at first glance, but it was hard. My parents had no savings, no pension and no retirement plan, but the pub trade was all they knew, so they had to keep going. I was 25 at the time, living with them in the small flat above the pub. They seemed to age much quicker the longer they were in the dying pub trade.

Then on 15 December 2005, at around one o'clock in the afternoon in a packed pub full of his best customers and many of his friends, my dad's life took another huge turn.

Picture this: a freezing winter's day, my dad – like a DNA fusion of Basil Fawlty from *Fawlty Towers* (charming, angry and erratic) and Victor Meldrew from *One Foot in the Grave* (happy in his misery and letting everyone know about it) – wielding the carving knife and silently daring people to ask for an extra slice of meat. The pub was heaving; everyone wanted to eat at one o'clock, which really used to annoy my dad because he could only use the table once at that time. He was in full stress mode. Nothing new so far.

But then he just stopped. He stared into space. He stopped and went vacant long enough that it became awkward. The customers queueing up were looking at each other. I was looking at my sister. It was like the music in the pub stopped, and the scene was on pause. He then started muttering to himself, then shouting aimlessly, then screaming, then wailing and squealing aggressively. He still had the long, sharp carving knife in his hand, and the whole pub was frozen and on edge like a scene in a Western bar before a shoot-out.

Dad was clearly very distressed, so I tried to talk to him, I looked him square in the face, but he couldn't see or hear me. I managed

4

to drag him through the bar, away from the customers and out to the front of the pub – not easy, as my dad was 17 stone, and most of that in his beer belly. I shook him. I shouted at him. I slapped him in the face. Nothing. By that time, many of the customers had congregated around the front bay window to watch the drama unfold, and my mum and sister ran out to try to help Dad.

Within minutes a reinforced police van pulled up, two policemen got out, and one who looked no older than 19 pulled a baton from his belt and beat my dad around his back and legs until he collapsed to the floor. They both piled on top of him and wrestled him onto his front, strapped him up, bundled him into the back of the van and took him away from us. He was later sectioned. I wasn't allowed to see my dad for many weeks, as he was in a high-security ward for the mentally ill. This was our first experience of my dad's bipolar disorder. We had no idea what we were in for.

Oh, and did I mention it was his birthday? What a present. I will remember 15 December forever, for the wrong reasons.

My dad worked hard his whole life and he made huge sacrifices to give me and my sister a good life – one he'd not had himself. He took us on holidays he couldn't really afford. He bought me all the best sports equipment to give me a chance at being good at something: cricket, rugby, golf. He struggled financially to put me through private school. He bought me my first car. He put a deposit down for my first house.

Yet, in that moment, all the thanks he had for his hard work was public humiliation and mental illness.

It was the worst day of my life, too. I can't begin to tell you the humiliation, guilt and shame I felt while it was all happening, and for a long time afterwards. I felt very responsible for what happened. Many people have told me it's not my fault, but I believe that part of what broke my dad down was the endless pressure turned to stress, and the dependence I had on my dad.

I was 25 but still fully reliant on my parents for everything. I was like a baby chick, sitting in the nest, mouth open, chirping away, begging for food. Selfish. Feed me. Feed me. Feed me. I'd made absolutely nothing worthy of my life, despite having all the chances, support and some talents. I was good at most sports, I got A grades, I was top of the year in art; I could turn my hand to many things, but I was good at nothing. Especially standing on my own two feet. Sad but true.

My life was going nowhere, and I knew it, but I was stuck. Dependent and reliant. I was powerless because I didn't know how to change or improve my life. It meant starting again. It meant going out on my own. It meant fear. It meant rejection. I had the comfort of falling back on what my parents had built for me. This was a false safety blanket. It was like a cot for a 25-year-old baby.

But looking back, 15 December 2005 was also the best day of my life. The single turning point. The fork in the road. The start of my new life. It was like I'd had no opportunities in the 25 years preceding this day. At least, that's how the victim mentality I had at the time perceived it.

What I couldn't see then, but is really clear to me now, is that it was the greatest opportunity of my life, presented to me in the disguise of pain.

My shame eventually turned into motivation, or rather desperation, and I started searching for something. I started tentatively at first, but I soon built up momentum and my search became breathless and relentless. I had no real clue what I was looking for but I needed something, now. Anything. There was no other option. I had no choice.

The one independent, responsible move I had made up to this point was working part-time as an artist. I worked weekends and night shifts at the pub and painted during the day and late into the night. Art was something I was good at, and it seemed that the more screwed up your art was, the better it would sell. I was pretty screwed up, so I reckoned I was on to something.

However, I didn't have much success selling my art, because I was an artist, not a salesperson. I rarely ventured out of Peterborough, in fact I rarely ventured out of my house, and so my art got darker and more insular the more I distanced myself from people and places. A rare venture out for me was to Cowgate, a semi-boutiquey street in Peterborough, where a new, privately-owned interior design and furniture shop had opened called Elements. It was minimalistic and high-end, and as it was recently opened, the walls were bare.

The owner, Mike Wildman, was friendly, and in a rare moment of courage (or maybe opportunity), I asked him if he wanted to see any of my work. He agreed, and the next day I took my portfolio in to show him. I think some of my work raised his eyebrows; dark is an understatement. I used to paint to heavy metal (or Radiohead for a bit of light relief), so you can imagine what it was like.

Mike sifted through my work and picked a few pieces out. He offered to hang them in his studio on a sale-or-return basis. I was stunned and nervously excited, I'd never had any of my art exhibited or seen publicly before. Could this be the start of a real career for me as an artist? Well, as it turns out, no. But I never could have imagined where it was going to lead. Mike played a big part in my change of direction, and I am eternally grateful to him for believing in me when I didn't believe in myself.

Over the next few years, I sold a few paintings through Elements – enough to just scrape by for a while. The brightest moments of my short art career were the calls from Mike. He'd always call me personally to tell me when a piece of my art had been sold. He would tell me about the buyer, and he'd pay me right away, 60 per cent of the sale. I would ride my bike to Cowgate, go in and he'd give me a cheque with a handwritten note.

This was all great, but it was actually just the start of the journey, maybe even a distraction – the real opportunity was hidden in plain sight.

Mike had been investing in property on the side while he was setting up his shop. This was 2003 to 2005, so the UK property market was buoyant and seemed like it would keep going up forever. For at least a year, he'd be suggesting, nudging and then nagging me to go to a local property meeting. To get into property. To invest.

'What do I know about property? I'm an artist' I would say. 'I don't have any money anyway.'

The truth was, I was scared. Scared of anything new, out of my little comfort blanket of security, which was ironic as I was far from comfortable, and I had a political, rage-against-the-machine hatred of 'corporate' and 'commercial' yuppies anyway. F★★★ you I won't do what you tell me. So I kept politely declining, staying in my little bubble of quiet desperation.

All that changed on 15 December. I still felt scared, lonely, insignificant and useless, but my attitude towards putting myself out there was totally different. I said, 'F★★★ it, I'll go to that property meeting. I'll see what all the fuss is about.'

Meeting the opportunity

It had been about a week since my dad's episode, and there was a monthly property meeting being held at the Holiday Inn. I was going, and I was scared. I got some cheap business cards printed, with the grandiose title 'Artist & Investor', and I rode my bike there in the freezing cold. There were a dozen or so people there, but I managed to sit on my own for most of the event at the back to avoid talking to anyone. I felt a fraud and knew nothing about property.

But Mike was in my head, nagging me: 'Rob, don't just go there and sit at the back on your own the whole night.' Just as I was heading out the door inconspicuously after the talk, something stopped me and I turned right into the bar instead. I'll stay for a bit, see what this is all about.

Looking back, I can see that my first attempt at networking was a giant cringe fest: no eye contact, nervous handshakes, cheap business cards thrust around (or rather hidden behind) as an excuse to exit the conversation. I got through everyone pretty quickly, leaving one last person sat at the bar on his own. I sat down and looked at him a couple of times, but he was just staring straight ahead, looking at the spirits hanging on the wall. We sat there in a long, awkward silence (for me).

I had racked up nearly £50,000 of consumer debt by this stage in my life, and even buying two drinks was a struggle. But I couldn't bear the silence anymore, so I moved closer to him.

'Do you want a drink?' I said.

'Diet Coke,' he said, completely deadpan, without even turning his head to look at me.

I bought the grumpy bugger a Diet Coke, slid it over to him, and reached out my hand.

'Hi, I'm Rob.'

Staring straight into my eyes without a hint of a smile, he replied, 'I'm Mark Homer. Good to meet you.'

He shook my hand so hard it made my whole body pop.

We exchanged pleasantries, I spouted a few property-related words to make it look like I knew what I was talking about, we exchanged business cards and we went about our respective lives. Or so we thought.

I was a bit despondent when Mike asked me how it had gone; I didn't feel like I'd gained anything from the event, and I felt out of my depth. He sat me down and explained that networking takes time. That you can't expect the people and the money to flock to you on day one. That the important part is the follow-up. That was terrifying – what would I say? Following Mike's advice, I held my breath, got out the small pile of business cards I'd collected, and emailed every single person to say it was nice to meet them, and to ask if there's anything I could help them with.

I can't remember exactly who replied, but the reply that interested me was the one from Mark Homer. He invited me to his office to meet his boss, who owned a property-sourcing company. He also suggested three books that were really good for property investing and 'personal development' (a term I'd never heard of before). This presented me with a quandary. I was hungry, motivated and desperate, and I really wanted to make a change, but I hated reading books. In fact, the last book I had read cover to cover was Roald Dahl's *Fantastic Mr Fox*, when I was probably nine years old.

Sure, it's a great book, but not great preparation for a meeting with two property tycoons. I wanted to impress these guys so, despite my painfully slow reading pace, I bought the books and got stuck in. I can't tell you why, or even how I read them all that week – it took me hours and hours, I'm one of those people who reads by saying the words aloud in my head – but I got through them all just in time for the meeting. And, to my surprise, I really enjoyed them!

I walked with a bit more swagger into the small but fancy new office, knowing I'd done my homework. Mark met me at reception, and right away he asked me about the books. I could recall a decent amount of the content, spat out a few fancy words to impress Mark, like assets vs. liabilities, yield, mastermind, and we engaged in one of the most stimulating conversations I'd had in my life. (I didn't know this at the time, but this was one of Mark's little tricks. He would recommend books to people as a kind of test to see if they actually read them, to see if they actually followed through. Years later, he told me that I was the only person he'd ever met who read all three books before meeting him again.)

The meeting went well, we got on and I felt like I'd impressed them. Their outfit looked slick. They looked successful, rich – it was a real business with multiple income streams and opportunities, and I wanted a piece of it. I left the meeting on a high, but then my imposter syndrome, victim mentality and chronically low self-worth kicked in. *What would these guys see in me?* I had no experience. No money. I was in debt. I was a struggling artist. Why would they be interested in me? I stewed on this for a while, did the usual process of beating myself up, but then had a brainwave: what if I offered to work for free? I could do a few shifts at Dad's pub, I could work weekdays for these property guys, and I could paint late at night like I was doing already.

I followed up again, and we arranged another meeting at their offices. Just as I was getting ready to give them my great idea, Mark said, 'We would like to offer you a job here. We can't pay much in salary, but we can pay big commissions for properties sold to investors.' I tried my best to hide my shock, awe and excitement, probably not very well, and I accepted the job on the spot. I knew what I wanted, and I would have worked for free anyway, so any money was a bonus. I was wildly excited about all the new opportunities headed my way, but then it hit me again – BANG. *I don't know anything about property. I've never sold anything in my life. I hate selling. Why would anyone buy from me? I'm just a skint artist.*

The result

Here's the radio edit of the next 15 years. I worked at that property company for just under a year, clearing my £50,000 debt and making just short of a net six-figure income. Mark and I forged a fantastic friendship that is still going strong to this day, and a business partnership that's stronger than ever. One of the proudest moments of my life was being best man at Mark's wedding, and he was also best man at mine.

We bought almost 20 properties together on the side in that first year, 2006, while working for the property-sourcing company. Mark and I owned them jointly, 50/50, and he and his mum and stepdad put up all the money. We set up our own deal-sourcing property company, which had a turnover of many millions of pounds. We then pivoted that business model into property training, and we have generated well in excess of £100 million in revenue since. We continued to build our own property portfolio, buying hundreds of rental units, virtually all with none of my own money, most of which we still own and get recurring income from to this day.

Our property portfolio grew to such a size that we needed our own lettings agency, which now manages nearly 1,000 rental units and is likely to become the biggest lettings agency in our city. As our property training business and brands grew, we attracted attention from other companies, and bought a personal development training company for a very small amount of money in a rescue package. We turned that business into a multimillion-pound company, which is still thriving today.

We currently employ almost 100 people in our offices, and around the same again outsourced around the UK. We won Business of the Year in 2016 and Property Training Company of the Year in 2017. I retired (financially) in my late 20s and became a millionaire before the age of 31. I tried my hand at retiring a good few times, but I couldn't stand it, and it rarely lasted more than a few weeks – just long enough to get itchy feet again.

The more opportunities that came my way, the more I seemed to want to grab them all. I'd spent 25 years taking hardly any, so I guess I was making up for lost time. I also started to enjoy greater and greater challenges, so when opportunities for public speaking came about, I grabbed them. I was both terrified and terrible at first, for many speeches, but I eventually broke three longest speech marathon world records: the individual speaking world record of 47 hours, and the team speaking world record of over 120 hours, twice.

I've written over a dozen books, some in partnership with my business partners and many others under my own name alone. Many of my books have become number-one bestsellers across all books categories. I am told *Money* was one of the top-selling finance business books of 2018–20 in the UK. I'm published by Hachette, the second largest global publisher behind Penguin, and they've been fantastic to work with.

I could never have predicted some of the things that have happened. My podcast, *The Disruptive Entrepreneur*, has had millions of downloads and subscribers in more than 200 countries. Better still, I've been fortunate to interview, meet and become friends with many of the most successful and famous people in the world, including celebrities, billionaires and the world's greatest achievers. I still pinch myself that such amazing and inspiring people view me with enough credibility to allow me into their lives, and I often feel slightly unworthy of their friendship.

Through all of this, my social media presence has compounded. I was one of the very first UK 'influencers' to get Facebook Supporter Program status – thousands of people now subscribe to my exclusive content – and then Facebook Stars, and then Facebook paid live events, and I was first in line for LinkedIn Live videos.

My property portfolio has given me the time and financial freedom to travel the world, and it has enabled my young son to play in various British, European and world golf championships. Possibly my greatest and proudest achievements (which aren't even mine!) are the eight holes-in-one (aces) my son hit by the age of eight. His first was when he was three, unofficially the youngest ever golfer to hit a hole-in-one, and his seventh and eighth were a week apart. Writing this does make me feel a little uneasy; it's uncomfortable to brag, or 'humble brag', about external achievements. But one of my mentors said to me, 'facts are facts, Rob, they are not brags'. All of these came about because I simply opened myself to new opportunities – right now, we're merging all of our companies into one brand, Progressive, and taking our events to a global audience. We are likely to go from 850 training days and events a year to many thousands, serving ever greater numbers of people. We are also developing around 150 units in our commercial to residential property portfolio and acquiring some companies to build our business portfolio, increase our reach and diversify our risk.

In the early years, I'll admit that money was important to me. Paradoxically, the more I've made, the less important it has become; helping others, doing meaningful work and making a difference has far overtaken it. Don't get me wrong, I still enjoy money, but I have got a greater sense of fulfilment and privilege from setting up the Rob Moore Foundation, to help underpriv-ileged and young people get a better financial education, and to start and scale their own enterprises. Mike gave me a shot and believed in me as an artist, and I want to be that person for many other budding entrepreneurs.

One single moment, disguised as the worst of your life, can turn out to create not just one opportunity, but every single opportu-nity for all the great things in your life there and forever after. That is the power of opportunity.

Despite the thousands of opportunities I missed, ignored, rejected or had been totally oblivious to, the next day, the next moment, the next nanosecond, another one always presents itself. I know this now, but I couldn't see this at the time. I was stuck. Blinkered. Consumed by my own self-pity. Walking around in a trance. Blind. Bitter.

Once you get your head out of your arse, where it's very dark and all you can see is shit, and start looking around you, in front of you and inside of you, it's amazing what you see. Then you realize it's been there all along. How were you so oblivious for so long?

Seize the day

I believe you win at life one day at a time. You positively dictate your future by owning the present, and the present is today. All success is created today. Seize today. Seize this moment. There is no tomorrow.

No matter how hard things are today, you always have tomor-row to start again; to seize the day, to win at life. You get way more attempts at success than you think, way more opportunities to win, way more chances to try. All you have to do is get through the day, to be able to seize today, every day.

Winning at life is all about taking opportunities and making decisions. Opportunities do not come once a month or once a week or even once a day. They come every second, every nano-second. They are infinite and limitless. Be aware of the infinite opportunities around you. Spot and then evaluate the ones that are right for you. Seize them today, and every other day, to win at life.

This is not another personal development or mindset book. In fact, I wrestled hard with my publisher (whom I love dearly) to ensure I didn't write A. N. Other mindset book, despite their desire for me to write a mindset book. I hope they don't edit this out because it's important. I wanted to write something different, something more unique, venturing into an area other authors have not explored. There was to be no swear word in the title, no subtle or magic art, and I'm not an ex-military, SEAL or SAS super-human-psycho. If you search 'opportunity' on Amazon or Audible, you'll find virtually nothing, yet to me that's exactly what life is all about: success, progress, growth, happiness, fulfilment is all about spotting and taking opportunities.

I want to thank my amazing business partner and best friend, Mark Homer. We both saw an opportunity, hidden in plain sight, that we both needed at the time but didn't know we did. We are 15 years in a partnership and still going on growing strong. We took a chance on each other. There was no proof. It was risky. We could have failed. Even to this day we have both experienced hard times and challenges that have threatened our partnership, but we are still growing and supporting each other. I'll share the full story later in the book as I believe it can really help you on your own journey of seizing opportunities.

Our partnership not only ranks up there in the best decisions of my life, but it has spawned hundreds of subsequent knock-on opportunities that have totally transformed my life in virtually all areas – health, wealth, growth and happiness. Who'd have thought such a grumpy ol' bastard could make such a profound difference to my life?!

Introduction

What is opportunity?

Opportunity can take many forms. Think about the last time you had an opportunity. How do you know it was an opportunity? What made it an opportunity for you?

> **Opportunity (noun):** a time or set of circumstances that makes it possible to do or achieve something.

Opportunity is many things to many people. It's a 'favourable or appropriate time, occasion or moment'. It's the apparent 'right set of circumstances'. It occurs at both '*the* right time' and '*your* right time'.

Opportunity is chance, and seizing that chance. It is luck, and making that luck. It's turning possibility into probability into actuality; it's turning fantasy into reality.

Opportunity is creating options and forging openings. Turning chances and choices into changes.

Opportunity is a new beginning – a fresh start again (… and again). It's another chance to succeed *this* time, or the *next* time, at *any* time. It's seeing a way forward. Seeking out a solution. Spotting what others are missing. Solving where others are struggling.

In business, opportunity is an 'exploitable set of circumstances with uncertain outcome, requiring commitment of resources and involving exposure to risk'.*

---

*This is the definition according to Businessdictionary.com.

It is about having faith in the infinite unknowns – the limitless, latent potential. It's found in the paradoxical balance of persistence and patience, in risking failure in order to succeed.

Opportunity is a window and a door; sometimes it opens right in front of you and sometimes it knocks, but it needs to be seen and to be taken in order to exist. It needs both a decision and a commitment.

Opportunity equals freedom: freedom from being trapped and out of control. Freedom to change. To move out of and away from stagnation, complacency, comfort or boredom. To embrace the unexpected: the change of plan, the curveball and the blind side.

It's a chance to improve, to grow, to learn new things and to do – and be – better than before, whether that's personally, in teams, in your family or for your health, wealth, happiness and business.

Opportunity is about *already* being ready. Putting yourself out there to meet the opportunity. Making things happen, not waiting for things to happen. Creating your own luck and seizing the day.

By definition, opportunity is a *thing: an opening, an event*, and you can choose what you do with it. You can see it or miss it, seize it or squander it, let it in or push it away, say 'no' to it or say 'hell yes' to it.

When I asked the 20,000 members (and counting!) of my Facebook group, the Disruptive Entrepreneurs Community, what opportunity means to them, their responses were enlightening, and they clearly showed that there's a big element of self-knowledge to opportunity: you need to know yourself and be ready before opportunity will appear, whether it's something that exists already or something new you create.

What you do with an opportunity can become part of its very definition – can an opportunity be real if you don't engage with it? 'If you can't see the opportunity it has no value or meaning,' said one person. 'Taking advantage of a set of circumstances that can give you a positive experience and result,' said another. Some talked about the opportunity existing already, waiting to be seen and grabbed: 'It's an external factor which, should you shape a course of action towards seizing it, could have a positive outcome', creating 'an unexpected (but not unwelcome) set of events or circumstances'. For others, opportunity is 'Something I have made for myself!'. 'It's something you create yourself and act on because you see and do what others can't and don't.'

People talked about opportunity being transient – if you don't take an opportunity, it disappears. Some think opportunity is something everyone sees but few take action on, others think it's hidden to most people. For some, opportunity is stronger in adversity – look at everything in life, especially failure, as an opportunity – that, conversely, 'success can be a poor teacher' and that you learn the most from your mistakes.

One thing many people agreed on was that taking action is key: when opportunity knocks, as the saying goes, you need to actually open the bloody door to make something happen. You need to wake up, be present, be ready, mentally and physically, to jump in or on at the right time.

The American entrepreneur Thomas Edison, arguably history's most persistent action taker, reputedly said 'the reason most people do not recognize an opportunity is because it usually goes around wearing overalls and looking like hard work.' I believe there is limitless, infinite opportunity hidden in plain sight.

Opportunity in abundance

For me, opportunity is in abundance. The only thing that changed for me in that moment, on 15 December 2005, was my state of mind: I was desperate, and I finally opened up to the opportunities around me, even if driven by pain. Since then, I've consistently seen that opportunity is everywhere – it's infinite.

Hindsight is always 20/20, of course, but if I look back to that day, to my turning point, I see it as a wormhole opening to a new state of being. I pivoted in that moment and turned into a different version of myself; I had opened my mind (or had my mind opened) to new opportunities that I'd never considered existed, and that I'd never seen, let alone knew were relevant or available to me.

With an open mind I could imagine myself and my life differently, I could see what was always there but hadn't been able to see – I wasn't stuck with a vision of myself as a struggling (and failing) artist, drowning in consumer debt and angry with the world.

Vision is such an important aspect of opportunity (we'll be coming back to this later): you have to (metaphorically) open your eyes to really see what's around you, as well as visualizing opportunities in order to create them.

And when you do open your eyes, you'll see that you're surrounded by opportunity. When I asked you at the start of this chapter to think of the last time you had an opportunity, was that moment right now? If not, then you're missing out. You have an opportunity RIGHT NOW, you just haven't seen it, recognized it or created it yet. That's what this book is going to help you do.

Of course, 'seeing' is subjective - you view from your own perspective, you're in your own context, with your own fears and failings, your own hang-ups and hardships, values and visions. But subjectivity can sometimes block opportunity - you can learn to step back and *really see* what's around you to spot the opportunities. To see what's actually there, not just what's coming through your 'opportunity filter'.

Our 'opportunity filters' are based on our judgements and past experiences, and we shouldn't blindly trust them. They're so often muddied by years of conditioning, self-doubt and imposter syndrome, and then sealed by our fears. You can learn to clean those filters and see what was really there all along. Just because you can't see it, doesn't mean it isn't there.

Then comes the moment to take action, to take that opportunity, to seize the day, and for this you need to cultivate a can-do attitude. That's often easy at the start – who hasn't been swept away at the beginning of a project, convinced it'll change everything? That life will be better 'when'. But maintaining momentum once the novelty has worn off and the fantasy becomes reality - this is where the progress and results show. For that, you need a grip on your routine, and I'll show you how to get that.

But you also need a desire or hunger to succeed, for something bigger than you; something to keep the fire inside you burning when things get hard. For me, at that key moment, it was desperation. I had to make it happen, because the alternative was just too painful, and I was ready to do anything to get it done. For so long I'd been sleepwalking, and finally I was awake. I was hungry (literally, being in £50,000 of consumer debt) and I had a strong desire to change my life.

That hunger and desire have to come with a dose of reality, though. You can't say 'yes' to everything. Rose-tinted filters won't help – if you consider every opportunity a blessing and something to take, or you find it hard to say 'no', you'll very soon be overwhelmed and unfocused. Your priorities will become unclear, you'll overstretch yourself, underperform, fail, let people down and then beat yourself up over it. I've seen this happen to many people – especially entrepreneurs, and I often wrestle with this myself, finding conflict and letting others down not natural to me.

Saying 'yes' became really trendy a few years back. In the British comedian Danny Wallace's book *Yes Man* (2005) he writes about a chance encounter with a man on a bus who told him people should say 'yes' more often. He saw this as an opportunity to change his life, and he decided to say 'yes' to everything for a year. Everything. Every offer, every invitation, every question. His adventure made for a hilarious book (and an equally hilarious film starring Jim Carrey) and it also kick-started the affirmative, optimistic yes movement.

But, as Wallace points out in his book, 'yes can go wrong.' Whether it's in business or dating or health or any other part of your life, saying 'yes' too much can create overwhelm, which makes you frustrated and even depressed, it can lead you to procrastinate and can erode your self-worth because you end up never finishing or achieving anything of any importance. I think there's a paradox in everything, and there's a clear one here: doing too much leads to achieving nothing at all.

All this might make opportunity seem complex and multi-dimensional, and it can be. Opportunity is within you as much as it is outside of you, and it's just as complex as you are. It's integrally linked to your innermost emotions; you take an opportunity when it feels right, you reject one when it doesn't – we'll dive into how your emotions manifest your opportunities in the next chapter. The key is knowing yourself and adapting yourself, managing your emotions – your filters, your attitudes and your approaches – to maximize your opportunities.

Yet it's also simple: it's something you see or you don't, something you take or you don't, something you create or you don't. It's the flip of a coin, a snap decision, a fleeting moment. And there's an infinite number of them.

In Part 1 of this book, we'll look more closely at opportunity, what it is and where it is, how it's related to luck and pure potentiality. We'll lay down the foundations you can build on to bring more opportunity into your life.

Then get ready to take notes and start practising and implementing because, when all is said and done, more is said than done. In Part 2, we'll look at how to prepare for opportunity – how to adapt and develop yourself and your own life areas in order to create the conditions to let opportunity appear.

In Part 3, we'll continue the practical approach and skill up on spotting, assessing and taking opportunities. This section contains practical advice to help you make real change, because to know and not to do is not to know.

Then roll up your sleeves and get out your calendar. In Part 4, I'll guide you through my tried-and-tested methods for seizing the day, from planning through execution to evaluation, and the continued up-scaling and up-cycling of ever greater opportunities and the gifts they bring to your life.

But how can seizing the day help you win at life? And what does that mean, anyway? In Part 5, we look more closely at success, progress and 'winning at life', helping you change your perspectives and leverage your opportunities in a way that works for you.

In Part 6, you'll make commitments and get some accountability for creating opportunities, seizing the day and winning at life. Start now. Get perfect later.

So, are you ready to welcome opportunity into your life?

Summary

Opportunity means different things to different people. By definition, opportunity is a *thing*, an opening, an event, and you can choose what you do with it. You can see it or miss it, seize it or squander it, push it away or let it in, say 'yes' to it or say 'no' to it. In this book, you'll learn the habits, skills and tactics to help you create, spot and take opportunities, seize the day and win at life.

TAKE ACTION

. . . .

What does opportunity mean for you?

1 Write down your own definition.
2 Write a list of situations or events in the last week that matched that definition, if you can think of any.
3 Put a tick or a cross next to each one to indicate if you took the opportunity or not.

We'll come back to this list a bit later.

PART I
Opportunity knocks ...

I

The 'nature' of opportunity

At what point would you say the probability of something happening is so small it's effectively impossible? One in a thousand? One in a million? In 2016, Canadian scientists did a study that showed we are terrible at understanding probability. So some of these statistics might surprise you.

We often use being struck by lightning as an analogy when we think something's extremely unlikely, but you actually have a 1 in 700,000 chance of it happening to you this year – that makes it about five times more likely to happen than being killed by a shark, and 500 times more likely than winning the lottery. You have a 1 in 10,000 chance of finding a four-leaf clover and a 1 in 8,000 chance of catching a shiny Pokémon (you know who you are). You're about 150 times more likely than that to become a millionaire.

But one thing makes all these unlikely events seem ordinary: you. Your very existence. You had a 1 in 5.5 trillion chance of being born. That's 1 in 5,500,000,000,000.

Think about it. For you to be born, your mother had to get pregnant, which means she had to meet your father (or at least an egg and sperm had to have a chance meeting and love affair!). And for that to happen, your parents also had to be born, which meant their parents had to meet, and so on going back for generations and generations. It's effectively a string of very rare and unlikely opportunities that led to your existence. Here. Now.

In fact, you can trace this probability all the way back to the beginning of life on Earth. Our planet was formed just over 4.5 billion years ago, and after about 500 million years, molecules started to bump into each other around the hot vents deep in the ocean. They would join together and break apart in endless combinations, until eventually some of them formed a little bubble, trapping other molecules inside.

Or maybe you're a proponent of the theory that the Earth was seeded from outer space – that meteorites from other planets brought those molecules to our planet and kick-started life?

However it began, this process went on for millions of years, and it led to the very earliest, simplest forms of life. Slowly, and against all the odds, these prehistoric cells started to divide and evolve, becoming bacteria, plants and, much later, animals.

The point is that you, and everything around you, is the result of a sequence of extremely unlikely events over millions of years. You represent a string of opportunities that were taken at exactly the right time, consciously or unconsciously, randomly or not so randomly.

Opportunity is in our biology

We have evolved to spot the opportunities that will keep us alive and help us produce the next generation. Think of animals: they sense opportunity. They see, hear or smell their prey. They notice and track down their potential mate. They spot the safe place to lay eggs. It's wired into us biologically.

That's still true for us humans today. Think about when you get an exciting opportunity – what does it feel like? Where do you experience it? Is it butterflies in your stomach, or a fizzing feeling that travels through your body, or a little tingle somewhere else ;-) ?

That could be down to adrenaline – the fight-or-flight hormone. When we feel fear, adrenaline floods our body to make us act. At a biological level, it wants us to run away from the scary thing, or fight it, in order to survive. We get that surge of adrenaline in life-threatening situations. Imagine someone trapped in a burning building with their unconscious child – it's adrenaline that gives them the strength to kick down a door and carry their child to safety.

But there are two sides to the adrenaline coin: one side is fear, the other is excitement. Have you ever heard an interview with a professional athlete right before a race? The interviewer asks, 'Are you nervous?' and the athlete often replies, 'I'm excited.' Turning their fear into excitement helps athletes perform better under pressure.

It's the same for public speaking. Getting up and talking in front of an audience takes the number-one spot on our list of fears … we're more scared of public speaking than of death! If you've been on stage, you'll recognize the adrenaline rush: for some people, it causes stage fright and makes them freeze, but others can redirect it and turn it into excitement.

I've done thousands of speeches in front of probably millions of people by now, and I've set two world records in public speaking, but that doesn't mean it's ever been easy or without nerves. At the beginning I was terrified. I remember getting sweaty palms the moment I agreed to do my first talk in front of a couple of hundred people. Every winner was once a beginner and every master was once a disaster, I told myself, and I got stuck into some really intensive training. One of the things I learned was that you can't just dismiss the fear and try to suppress the adrenaline; you need to turn it to your advantage.

This approach is backed by research. In 2014, Harvard psychologists showed that people who told themselves 'I am excited' before getting on stage gave better speeches than people who told themselves 'I am calm'. It's even got a name: anxiety reappraisal. It's the process that helps you turn fear into opportunity. This is a vital transfer of energy and a tactic you can implement in many areas of your life.

As humans, we have an additional dimension to dealing with opportunities. We are conscious beings, so we can apply language to opportunities, we can use reason and logic, we can create the conditions that nurture more, different or new opportunities. (We'll look at this in depth in Part 2 – get your highlighters ready.)

While life-threatening situations happened daily in our ancestors' lives, they're not actually that common these days. Yet we still get that surge of adrenaline when faced with an opportunity, like our life still depends on it. It could be something as small as an incoming email that makes your heart race – is it an offer for that job you applied for? Or catching someone's eye in a busy pub – could they be attracted to you too?

The hormonal surge can be addictive. Some of us crave it – we have 'shiny penny syndrome', we like the rush of a new opportunity and the excitement of what might happen if we take it. This could be in new courses you take and businesses you set up, new jobs you go for or new life partners.

- An entrepreneur might jump on an emerging trend and create a whole new industry, like Facebook or Uber; another might spend all their time starting new projects, never following through or finishing anything, starting again and again and again to get that fix.
- A man might spot his ideal partner across a crowded bar, jump on the opportunity to ask them out and live happily ever after (I'll tell you that story later...); another might constantly seek the butterflies and continually seek new relationships, creating chaos and loneliness, even affairs or addictions.
- A parent might nurture a single passion and skill in their daughter and take the opportunity for her to enter computer coding competitions, giving her a head start and talent in a dynamic field; another might push her in many directions, trying to get her to take every opportunity available and ultimately overwhelming or burning her out.

- A woman might take the opportunity to get fit by training with a local football club, winning the league; another might chase every new fitness fad, app, tool, scheme and celeb, never finding what really works for her.

These people all had access to the same opportunities, but a number of things set them apart. They take the *right* opportunity at the *right* time and focus on making sure they succeed. They know *which* opportunities to take, and which ones to pass. We'll look in depth at every step of that process in Part 2.

The important thing to take away here is that we are hardwired for opportunity. Biologically, we can spot opportunities and we're prone to seek the rush they bring over and over: the newness, the optimism, the hope, the exploration and the growth.

Which means you're not stuck or trapped the way you are. If you think you're not good at spotting opportunities, or you can't overcome fear and turn it into excitement, or you don't know how to stop chasing all the shiny stuff, you *can* change. You're just one decision away. There's something else going on in our brains that lets us adapt and develop.

When we learn, when we're exposed to new things and train ourselves to adjust to new approaches, we are literally rewiring our brains. This is possible because of neuroplasticity – the ability to change the connections between brain cells, changing and creating new circuits in our brains.

There is still a lot we don't know about this process, but research has suggested that our experience drives these changes, and that it's possible to train our brains in many different ways. This is important to acknowledge about yourself: you *can* change, and you can create new habits. You are not destined to live out your parent's life or old conditioning and triggers that recur in your present. You are not your past, and the past does not have to dictate the future. A lot of what we'll look at in Parts 2 and 3 in this book will be about retraining ourselves to create, spot and take (new) opportunities.

Opportunity captures our imagination

Opportunity fascinates us humans. It's not surprising, considering how fundamental it is to our biology. Think about the last novel you read or film you watched. There was probably a turning point in the story where the main character was faced with an opportunity: a choice, a quandary or a fork in the road. Think of the moment when Luke Skywalker gets a message from Princess Leia through R2D2. Or when Neo receives cryptic messages about 'The Matrix'. Or when Dorothy follows the yellow brick road to Oz.

This is part of the hero's journey – the call to adventure. It forms a fundamental part of the *human* stories we know and love because opportunity appeals to us, not only to our biology but to our imagination. We wonder what we might do if we were them, or what might happen if they didn't take the opportunity.

This isn't a modern thing, opportunity has featured in our cultural history for centuries. In fact, opportunity was a mythical person in Greek and Roman civilization – Kairos in Greek and Tempus (meaning 'time') in Latin. In ancient Greece, a statue of Kairos stood at the site of the first Olympic Games, to remind athletes and spectators that opportunity is about timing. They were smart people, those ancient Greeks. Time waits for no one, and neither does opportunity.

Opportunity and time

In this book, you'll read a lot about time – the importance of speed, fast and measured thinking, making quick decisions, taking time to research and how to manage your time to maximize opportunity. I think that's down to this intrinsic link between time, timing and opportunity.

As we saw in the Introduction, time is a fundamental element of opportunity, intrinsic to its very definition: a time or set of circumstances that makes it possible to do or achieve something. Not just *what* the opportunity is, but *when* the opportunity is.

Opportunity is also a thing – something that exists, whether or not we create it, spot it or take it.

The way we view and use time can shape our opportunities. In his podcast *Akimbo*, the US marketing guru Seth Godin, a rare double guest on my podcast *The Disruptive Entrepreneur*, says, 'Time is one of the only things that is under our control.' He believes we have choices about how we use our time – he asks, 'Are you going to pass the time or spend the time?'

He talks about something called Stone Age Economics: if you had a Stone Age baby today, Godin reckons it would grow up to be indistinguishable from everyone else. But in its own context, thousands of years ago, it would have grown up to spend a few hours a day running around and hunting, spending its time and energy surviving, and relaxing the rest of the day.

Now, he says, we spend our time like it's a resource. This makes opportunity cost important: whenever we spend time, we're not only making a decision about how to spend that time – what opportunity to take, but also how *not* to spend it – what to say 'no' to.

This links back to the appealing, shiny nature of an opportunity – the rarer it seems, the more finite the possibility, the more appealing it is. It's actually the finite nature of time, basically the fact that we're all going to die eventually, that makes opportunity so exciting. And often so scary.

This link to time is also what causes so many people so much stress around opportunity (I have loads of solutions to this, which we'll get to in Part 3). I bet you've wished for more time, more hours in the day, that time would stop or at least slow down.

But imagine if it did … you'd be miserable. Why? You'd be bored out of your mind, because with unlimited time, opportunity cost goes down. There's no thrill anymore because you can do everything – you have the time.

Think of Connor MacLeod in *Highlander*: he's immortal and, sure, he gets the thrill of trying to survive while everyone's waving swords around his head, but over the centuries he's seen everything, he's taken opportunities, missed opportunities and noticed that it all comes back around eventually. He's missing the finite nature of human life that we all need to kick our arses occasionally. As Godin says, 'We are emotionally hooked on making this choice about how we use our time.' Without that, we lose the thrill.

The Stoic philosophers of ancient Rome, like Seneca and Marcus Aurelius, were constantly reminding their followers of the finite nature of time, later summed up in the motto *memento mori*. It's Latin for 'remember that you must die'. You can find it all over the place in sculptures, paintings and writings – like Kairos, it's there to remind us not to pass up opportunities, not to waste our time … not to just pass it with our feet up in front of Netflix (although I do love a good documentary).

If you found out that you only had a year to live, what would you do? Take a minute to write down a list.

Now look at it. Is there anything on your list that you're holding back on doing because you're scared? Is there anything you're putting off until another time?

Go through the list and underline the things you'd do if you had only a month to live. Do those things reflect the priorities in your life? Think about what you're actually doing now, with your life stretched out in front of you. Are you focusing on your priorities?

If you're not, it's not end of story. You don't have to close this book, criticize yourself and carry on, business as usual. Realizing there's a gap between your real life and your ideal life is, in itself, an opportunity, and in the coming chapters I'll help you work out how to close that gap. Tomorrow is always a new day, and there's always a new way.

The many faces of opportunity

Now we've established that, by nature, we want to take action when there's opportunity, and that we connect to opportunity with our senses and through our consciousness. And we need all of those senses, all our faculties, to create or notice or grab opportunities, because opportunity comes in many different forms.

Have you ever looked back and realized that something that had happened – and perhaps passed you by – had been an opportunity, but you hadn't recognized it in the moment? That with hindsight, through the lens of time, you could look at the situation differently and see it for what it was?

Opportunity is a thing but, like everything, it exists through our own subjective perception. It isn't just how it is – it's how you see it, how you hear it, how you smell or taste or feel it.

There's a lot of research and theorizing about opportunity *discovery* versus opportunity *enactment*. Is opportunity just an object waiting for us to discover it and take it, or is it something we create, something that comes from our own perceptions and experiences?

I think it's both of those things. We'll come back to this in more detail soon, but for now, I want to lay down the idea that opportunity comes in various forms and manifestations.

This is something many people have talked about. In his 1937 book *Think and Grow Rich* (which I totally recommend), the US self-help writer Napoleon Hill wrote, 'Opportunity often comes disguised in the form of misfortune, or temporary defeat.' I think many opportunities hide in the shadows of challenges and problems, mistakes and events that people perceive to be bad luck. I've interviewed a lot of big entrepreneurs on my podcast, *The Disruptive Entrepreneur,* and when I ask them where they get their ideas for a business, where they find opportunity, how businesses can succeed, they almost always talk about what we too often see as negatives.

There's a lot of negative language and sentiment around failure, mistakes, problems and challenges, but the truth is that, without these, we wouldn't have any success, in any aspect of our lives. You have to fail to succeed. You need a problem to find a solution. You have to kiss a few frogs to find a prince or princess.

There are endless stories about people who have built empires on mistakes (take Richard Branson, for example) and we'll look at some of those in the course of this book.

Now hopefully I've started to paint a picture of opportunity for you ... it might look like a Jackson Pollock painting at this stage, but over the next few chapters we'll clarify it a bit more and start to make sense of what form and function opportunity has in our lives.

Spoiler alert: you're surrounded by opportunity right now.

Summary

As conscious animals, we are hardwired to respond to opportunity. It captures our imagination and, as a concept, has been part of our culture for thousands of years – reminding us of its fleeting nature and intrinsic link to time. Opportunity has many manifestations and can be disguised, hiding in the shadows of our darker moments.

TAKE ACTION
. . . .
Make your One Year to Live List.

If you haven't already done this exercise earlier in the chapter, take the time now to write down all the things you would do if you found out you only had a year to live. This isn't a bucket list (let's face it, those only ever make us feel shit), it's a *realistic* list of how you would ideally change your life.

Next, underline all the things you would do if you only had a month to live.

Take some time to examine your list compared to the life you're living right now. Do your priorities match your values?

2

Opportunity is everywhere

I mentioned in the previous chapter that opportunity is often disguised. I'm sure you've experienced this, because I know I have. It's just we never know it until we look back through the lens of 20/20 hindsight.

When I was a poor, tortured artist, drowning in debt and angry with the world, holed up creating pieces I didn't even know if anyone would want, and listening to the only music that seemed to match my mood – heavy metal (which I still love today, to be fair) – I wouldn't have spotted an opportunity if it hit me in the face. I'd decided that there were no galleries in Peterborough, and I didn't like London, so there was no way I could show my work. No chance. No opportunity.

What a load of crap I was telling myself.

Looking back at that now, I can see it so clearly: there are loads of ways I could have found the art lovers in Peterborough (because they do exist, honestly!). I could have gone to Cambridge or Birmingham or any other nearby city and found art galleries. I could have met with local artists and art dealers, networked, made connections. I could have sucked it up and gone to London, a city filled with art and art lovers. Sure, I might have been poor, but a bus trip doesn't cost much … and I could have jumped on my push bike and cycled there for free in less than a day.

Opportunity was dressed up as hard work. As pain. As anger. As fear. It was all around me, but I wasn't ready to see it.

For years, my dad was nagging me to buy houses. But what was he on about? Me, buy a house? Who was he kidding?! That was ridiculous. Instead, I watched the opportunity double the money in someone else's pocket, right in front of my eyes, year after year.

Nothing changed to that opportunity in the years I watched it without taking it; the only thing that changed was me when I eventually took it.

For years, I kept myself to myself, I didn't get out there and network. There were property meetings going on all the time, but I never went. Week after week, that opportunity whizzed by, cloaked in fear. My fear. What would people think about me, some bloke with no money and no experience, rocking up to buy a house? With what? I felt like a joke. Until I swallowed my fear and pride and went to one, only to meet my business partner who I would go on to make hundreds of millions of pounds with.

Those opportunities were always there, right in front of me. I stared right at them, but I didn't see them for what they were. I saw the opportunity to exhibit my art as an obstacle; I saw the opportunity to buy a house as an impossibility; I saw the opportunity to network and meet my business partner as fear. I saw them all, not for the opportunities they were but for their disguises – disguises I was giving them. I wasn't ready.

Maybe it makes sense. It takes a huge amount of strength to process the world when you see opportunities for what they really are, because they are all around us. Literally. Every way you look, every direction, around every corner, in every situation, in your problems and fears and failures, in your hopes and dreams and desires. Once you open the floodgates, you realize opportunity is infinite. And it's not just the opportunities that are there already; it's the ones you can create and mould, the ones you can imagine and manifest.

Opportunity is endlessly abundant for all of us. We just have to be ready to see it.

A world of opportunity

Have you ever played the Six Degrees of Kevin Bacon game? You have to name a celebrity and work your way back to Kevin Bacon in less than six moves. Julia Roberts is one move, because she was in *Flatliners* with Kevin Bacon. Kevin Hart is two moves – he was in *40-Year-Old Virgin* with Steve Carell, who was in *Crazy, Stupid, Love* with Kevin Bacon. You get the picture.*

The point is that this game is based on the theory that every person on the planet is connected in six moves or less. That network of connection has always provided abundant opportunity, and I've experienced this first hand. I interview a lot of big-name guests on my podcast, *The Disruptive Entrepreneur*, and many of them come through connections – people who follow me know people who know people, or friends of friends, or business partners of business partners. Those connections can be fired up fast – it takes a few seconds to send a WhatsApp message or an email. And each of those connections is an opportunity.

Life is all about people, connections, relationships. Those opportunities have always been there. But the exponential development in technology has added a new dimension, multiplying the already limitless opportunities around us.

With digital communication happening at the speed of light, opportunity has accelerated. We don't have to physically go and talk to someone, or post a letter, or even pick up the phone. Thanks to the internet, you can be living in the English countryside, find out about a job in New York, apply for it and do an interview without ever stepping on a plane. You can swipe right and meet the love of your life without taking off your slippers, let alone leaving the house. You can work out with the world's top personal trainers from the comfort of your own home, for a fraction of the usual cost. You can set up a charity with a partner in South Africa and producers in Germany to save lives by providing clean water in disaster zones in Asia.

---

*Incidentally, the Kevin Bacon game was itself an opportunity in disguise for its star. Kevin Bacon hated the game at first, but eventually saw it as an opportunity to make a positive impact in the world. He set up a charitable foundation called SixDegrees.org, which uses the theory behind the game to help people become celebrities for their own causes and has helped set up charities around the world since 2007.

Once you're open to it, you'll see opportunity at every turn.

And that's only opportunity that already exists. As I mentioned in the previous chapter, there's discussion about whether we take existing opportunities or create new ones – opportunity discovery versus opportunity enactment. The debate is particularly around entrepreneurship.

One theory is something called the individual–opportunity nexus. US researchers Jonathan Eckhardt and Scott Shane believe that, in business, opportunity exists objectively, despite claims that entrepreneurs create opportunities. They say it's the entrepreneur who shifts and changes until they land on an opportunity, which is there, fixed, objective. It might look like entrepreneurs are being creative, they say, but it's actually a process of (re)searching: opportunities exist to be discovered and exploited.

But when researchers asked a group of entrepreneurs about where their ideas came from, the opposite picture emerged: opportunities appeared as a result of the ways the entrepreneurs had made sense of their experiences. Rather than discovering static opportunities, they actually imagined them through the things that they did and the connections they made with people.

This shows a strong link between opportunities and ideas. There's a creative element to opportunity – it requires imagination, visualization, even dreaming. If you paint a clear enough picture, you can make your imagined situation so real that your mind can't tell the difference and it starts to change the way you act, which changes the way you live, which ultimately changes your situation. We'll come back to this in Chapter 3, but I'll say for now that it's not as woo-woo as it might seem.

There might be a two-sided debate here, but I don't think it's black and white – I don't think there's one right answer. I think the reality is a combination of the two viewpoints: that opportunities exist and they are created, that we discover some and imagine others. The better you are at the skills involved in both of those scenarios, the more opportunities you'll have. (We'll focus on those skills in Part 2.)

A big factor in all of this is mindset. There's a lot to say about mindset and success (I've written a whole book on it!) but I won't dive in too deep here. What I do want to point out is that the world is being filtered through our experiences, our biases, the inner critics in our heads, our assumptions and our beliefs. Whether we're aware of it or not, we're constantly attracting some things and repelling others. We're ready to see and take certain opportunities, and we're hiding from others.

Working on mindset can help adjust your filters. With an optimistic mindset, you might be able to see more opportunities around you without focusing on the problems. With the right approach to a pessimistic mindset, you can identify a negative and turn it into an opportunity.

One thing we'll revisit is the entrepreneurial mindset. Whatever area of your life you're looking at – it could be love or work or health or finance – adopting an entrepreneurial mindset can provide a strong basis for the skills you need to seize opportunities. And once you get that mindset, once you unlock the ability to create and spot opportunities, you'll really start to see that you're surrounded by them.

I did, and I wanted to understand what was really going on. That's what I want to share with you next.

Summary

Opportunity is all around you, you just need to adjust your filters to see it properly. Opportunity is both something that exists objectively and something you can imagine and create – learning the skills involved in both and changing your mindset can open up a world of limitless opportunity.

TAKE ACTION
. . . .
Write a list of your disguised opportunities.

In the Introduction, you wrote down a list of the opportunities you've had in the last week. Looking back at that list, are there things you've missed? Focus on today, right now. What opportunities do you have that are disguised as something else? Write down five opportunities and their disguises. Is there a pattern?

3
Visualizing opportunity

As you've gathered by now, I was a bit of a stubborn bastard when I was younger (ahem) and ignored all the advice I was getting to take the opportunities that were right in front of me. When I did start taking them, I soon levelled up on life and business. Success followed success. I believe a lot of that was down to me getting started on my personal development journey.

I had a breakthrough year in 2006 – business was going strong, I was making money and slowly getting used to not being a struggling artist. I had noticed that opportunities seemed to be appearing, and I was really interested in the spiritual dimension of what I was going through.

I was hungry for success, I wanted to win, to push harder, make more money, create more value, get to the next level, and the next. But I was also aware that my hunger could easily come across as desperation.

I was studying the law of attraction, reading Gregory Garcia's *The Secret: Law of Attraction* and exploring the ideas behind manifestation, looking for easier ways to attract results and people into my life than just the hustle and graft. This wasn't me being lazy (although I think it is for some people ... if that's you, here's my message: you can manifest all you want, but without doing anything you won't get anything). In fact, I sometimes tried too hard, and sometimes that really hard effort can come across as desperation. I don't think people are attracted to desperation. Think about being on a date with someone who seems really desperate. Not particularly hot, is it? It doesn't make you want to leap under the covers with them. I was just starting out in business and I wanted to succeed. I was, in fact, desperate for success, but I didn't want people to sense that, I didn't want to put them off.

One day I was chatting to Nick Hillson, an amazing designer friend of mine who was also into personal development at the time. I told him about my quandary, and he recommended I read something by Deepak Chopra. I picked up a copy of *The Seven Spiritual Laws of Success*, and it's probably not over the top to say it completely changed the way I think. That's where I first discovered the theory of pure potentiality.

The Law of Pure Potentiality

Let's pause here for a minute. As interested as I was in the whole idea of manifestation and the law of attraction – 'just visualize that dream life and it'll appear as if by magic, right in front of your eyes' – I wasn't convinced. I didn't go in for the woo-woo of it all. I needed something more solid, something more theoretical. Pure potentiality filled that gap for me.

The Law of Pure Potentiality is the first spiritual law of yoga. One of the first yogis to bring the practice to the West in the first half of the 20th century, Paramahansa Yogananda, is quoted as saying 'We are all the masters of each moment' – and I think this is a really good explanation for the theory.

According to the Law of Pure Potentiality, we are all pure awareness at our core. This realm, as it's described, is where our intuition, balance and harmony exist. It's the source of our creativity. It's the essence of our consciousness. It's the home of opportunity.

We are connected to every other person through this realm of pure awareness, so the theory goes. To tap into it, all we have to do is stop, be still, access the silence and just be. Simple, right? It's part of different Eastern philosophies and has been practised for millennia – in yoga, the mantra is *Om Bhavam Namah*, which translates as 'I am absolute existence' or 'I am a field of all possibilities'.

The idea is that if we can quieten ourselves and tap into that pure energy at our core, then anything is possible.

Bear in mind that I was pretty far away from yogi status when I started reading about this. I had tried a bit of meditation, but I ditched it pretty fast because I got so bloody bored. I'm a quick thinker, a quick mover, I take action, so trying to get me to stop and smell the roses was no mean feat.

But something about this really resonated with me. It flicked a switch in my brain of infinite possibility, infinite potential, limitless opportunity. It was a real mind opener for me, and I felt that I had to explore it more deeply. Then I got busy building my business and it stayed there, intriguing me in the back of my mind.

One thing I did kick into gear was visualization. After reading Napoleon Hill's *Think and Grow Rich*, I started putting the so-called law of attraction into practice. In his book, Hill writes about creating a 'mastermind group'. Not a real, physical one, where people meet and share experiences and so on, but an imaginary one.

In a mastermind group in your mind, you close your eyes and visualize a problem or a challenge or a goal or a desire. You create a boardroom scenario in which you've got elders and sages – people who are successful in different walks of life who you may feel could give you great advice on your problems or goals – all sitting around a table in your imagination. This isn't as easy as it sounds, and you really have to spark your imagination and inner child to visualize these people in your imaginary boardroom.

Once they're all there waiting for you, you go in and put your topic to them, whether it's a problem or challenge, or a goal or desire. Then you let them talk – you imagine the discussion, you visualize the debates, the different perspectives and opinions. And you imagine the different solutions they might bring to the table.

This exercise became something I did quite regularly, along with a daily mantra that I recited in my head every night when I went to bed (and still do, to this day … unless I fall asleep too fast, which is annoying). Come and lie down next to me – I'll take you through it (if you've seen some of my more intimate Facebook Lives, you'll be able to picture it too, ha-ha!).

I put my head on my pillow, close my eyes and recite my mantra: 'wealth, success, health, strength, happiness, confidence, non-judgement, abundance, love and gratitude'. Then I visualize my goals and my vision, then my challenges, my quandaries, my problems. I visualize solutions to them. Sometimes these come in words, sometimes in pictures in my mind.

This technique has been wildly powerful for me in terms of getting results – I believe this has been a key factor in attracting the results and the goals and the people I want into my life.

What works for me might not work for you, but what's the harm in trying? You need to lie down eventually anyway. Remember though, visualizing won't get you very far on its own. It has to be matched with a go-getter attitude, with putting yourself out there and positioning yourself in the right way. You have to ask for things (because if you don't ask, you don't get – we'll come to that). Just f★★★ing do it, be prolific rather than perfect, treat people well and give in order to receive. Visualization isn't a magic bullet, but in my experience it has an amazing power that I really wanted to explore.

So back to the story: we were in 2006 when I started to visualize, fast-forward at least a decade to a chat I was having with another good friend of mine, Matt Januszek. Matt owns Escape Fitness and has a great podcast (called *Escape Your Limits*); we have a lot in common and we meet up a few times a year. When we meet, we usually go to Wagamama and talk about the books we're reading and the podcasts we're listening to and the people who are inspiring us. This one particular time we met, he recommended I check out Dr Joe Dispenza. Matt had experienced a mindset shift that had left a big impression on him after reading some of Dr Dispenza's work. Like me, he was into visualization and, through Dispenza, he had discovered a new layer to make it even more powerful.

When people meditate or recite mantras or practise the law of attraction, they will usually visualize images and situations, or they might say words out loud or in their minds. But there is something missing in this: emotion. According to some of the thinkers in this space, including Dispenza, emotion creates energy, which creates a higher vibration. The theory goes that the more you put yourself in the emotional state you desire to be in, or that you would be in if you were to achieve the results you want, the higher you lift your frequency and the vibration of energy. That activates attraction through something called the 'unified field'.

This is where they borrow some ideas from science. Dispenza is a chiropractor and he's interested in all sorts of scientific fields, so he often refers to ideas in neuroscience and, in this case, physics.

Let's dive into it a bit. Albert Einstein first described the unified field theory as a way to connect his general theory of relativity, which explains gravitation, with electromagnetism, which is the interaction between electrically charged particles. Scientists have been working on the theory for over a century, and it's constantly developing in theoretical physics, but they're still looking for an answer, a physical law that connects everything.

What Dispenza and others have taken from this is the notion of connection – that everything is connected through forces and particles and vibrations, and that there are infinite possibilities at every point in time and space. They believe we can tap into this. Combined with the ideas from Eastern philosophy like pure potentiality, this becomes the foundation for a different way of thinking about opportunity – that through visualization and high-energy emotion, we can have a real effect on the world around us. This means we can open up new possibilities.

I haven't yet mastered meditating for eight hours a day in my pants in my living room, I haven't had billionaires knocking on my door without me ever leaving the house, and I haven't had offers to buy the companies I want for a pound without lifting a finger. (By the way, if you have a course on that, sign me up.) But I've been open to some of these ideas, and recently, I've focused on creating emotion in my body, imagining how I will feel and creating a higher vibration of energy, a higher frequency.

As I've mentioned, my default mode of being is hard work, graft and hustle – my dad raised me that way, he had me working from the age of six, earning a pound a week cleaning up in the pub after the busy night before and restocking the drinks shelves – and I think that's key to making the most out of visualization and approaches like this.

But, on the other hand (because there's always a paradox), I think hard work alone won't get you where you want to be. Sometimes graft is counterproductive because it wears you down, you end up making mistakes because you've burned yourself out. You can come across as a bit desperate. You need a balance of hard work and smart work. Visualization has really helped me do this.

It would probably be fair to say that when it comes to the Ferraris I've bought, the amazing celebrities and successful people and billionaires I've met and interviewed, the solutions I've found to many of my biggest problems and fears, the companies I've built, the books I've written, the podcasts I've created, the personal brand I've built and the world records I've achieved, I can put a good amount of my success down to my continual visualization and mantras and imagining a clear desired outcome.

The science of visualization

Why does it work? Pure potentiality and unified field theory aside, there has been some psychological research into why visualization seems to work for some people.

First, as I've mentioned before, the brain can't always tell the difference between a real memory and one we've visualized. A study led by researchers at Harvard showed that there's a tight link between remembering the past and imagining the future. Both use the same brain networks – we use the same process to look back and project forward.

This has all sorts of implications for how our memory impacts on our problem solving, for example. But it may also explain why visualization works. When we visualize, if we're using our brains in the same way as when we remember, we might be treating our visualizations the same way as our memories. We might trust them and build our confidence around them. This could help us overcome fear and take action towards our goals.

There's a link here to hypnosis – that if we visualize doing something we believe we can't do, we might be able to override our limiting beliefs and make it happen.

But the best analogy I've come across is likening visualization to tuning into a radio frequency. There's a saying that thoughts become things, and where attention goes, energy flows and results show. We see this externally in our lives all the time – the things we focus on are the things that change; the things we prioritize are the things that do the best. If we want to get fit, we're more likely to succeed if we make that a priority and focus on, say, strength training and cardio rather than watching every episode of *Game of Thrones*. The same happens internally, in our minds. We are more likely to achieve a goal if we tune our radio into the frequency we want; if we direct our thoughts and energy towards that priority, rather than letting them fly around all over the place and letting our emotions and fears take over.

Ready to dive even deeper? Some people believe this is connected to a part of the brain called the reticular activating system (RAS). The RAS is a network of brain cells that controls many different fundamental systems in our brains and bodies, and it's involved in the fight-or-flight response we looked at in Chapter 1. Some have claimed that the RAS acts as a filter – that it picks up on cues in our environment and feeds us more of the things we're focused on, which would explain why we get more of what we visualize.

However, the more likely explanation is psychological and has to do with goal setting. When we set a goal, the more specific it is, the more 'pull' it has – the more we move towards it. You've probably heard of SMART goals (specific, measurable, achievable, realistic and time-bound). They work because we have a clear guideline for what needs to be done. Add a visual dimension to that – and, even stronger, an emotional dimension – and the pull becomes unavoidable, even if it's unconscious.

It turns out this isn't just a weird quirk I share with Napoleon Hill – visualization does seem to work. In a month-long experiment, US researchers showed that visualizing their 'best possible selves' had a more positive effect on people than practising gratitude. In another study, people who *imagined* a positive future were significantly more likely to *expect* a positive future.

This impact on mood, optimism and expectations could help explain the results of visualization – as we'll see in later chapters, mindset is critical to seizing opportunities.

Imagining and realizing the future

Unlike the traditional SMART goal, visualization doesn't have a fixed timeframe. You can visualize exactly what you want, and in my experience you can make it a reality, but there's no way of knowing exactly when or where you will manifest it. I do believe that I can manifest the results that I want. I've got big plans and huge things happening that I can't share yet, but I'm not in control of the timeframe.

Sometimes I do set specific goals for things, like wanting to make an extra million pounds in the next X weeks. But it doesn't always happen that way. And this is where it's been a bit challenging for me in the past. There has to be a certain amount of letting go and accepting what *is* as well as striving for what you *want*. That's a quandary and a balance, and it's something I'm continually learning. I haven't reached full yogi status just yet.

A lot of this is about having faith and letting go. It's highly theoretical, and a lot of it is pretty controversial and disruptive. At this stage, I'm still researching what's going on in the universe and what my place in it all is. The more I know, the more I realize I don't know. I'll be learning for the rest of my life, probably without ever touching the sides of the power of it all.

Because how do I put into context the results I've had in my life and where they came from? Is it down to luck? What, even, is luck? Is it creating opportunity? Is it attraction or is it hard work? Is it having a clear vision? I'm piecing this all together, and there's a lot more work to be done on it – the thought leaders in this space have more to work out, and as our knowledge of psychology and neurobiology and the universe develops, we'll understand better where it fits in the story of opportunity.

What I know for sure is that each of us has more potential than we're using. There are constantly missed opportunities and chances passing us by. To really seize the day and win at life, we have to adjust ourselves. We have to learn and adapt and change. We have to have faith and patience as well as grit and an ethic of hard work. We have to overcome fear and find confidence, be optimistic and believe in ourselves.

There's no doubt in my mind that visualization plays an important part in that. It taps into my potential, shifts my mindset, tunes my radio into my priorities, and energizes the connections that can lead to what we might otherwise refer to as luck.

Summary

Visualization is a powerful tool for creating opportunity – especially if you bring in the emotion associated with your goal or desire. A mastermind group in your mind is a specific kind of visualization that can help you find solutions you didn't know you could imagine. There are lots of theories used to explain the power of visualization, including pure potentiality and unified field theory, and psychological research has shown it can have a positive impact on mindset – the key to harnessing opportunity.

TAKE ACTION

• •

Create a visualization you come back to at least once a day.

Write it down, draw it or create a vision board. Think about including these elements:

- a *mantra* that you repeat – a series of words that could be a positive affirmation, a goal or something you want to focus on
- an *image* of something you desire or want to achieve – it could be a house or a car, a partner, a family, a holiday or a skill
- an *emotion* – how will you feel when you achieve your goal? Try to recreate that feeling throughout your visualization.

4

The role of luck in opportunity

When I was a skint artist, I'd got myself into a big financial hole – I was up to nearly £50,000 in consumer debt, and that didn't include my mortgage on my house. I got to the point where the interest payments on my debt added up to more than I was earning as an artist, so I decided to sell my car. My car cost £10,000, and I had a five-year loan on it at £250 a month, which was a lot of money for a chap in his early 20s. I sold the car for £3,500, and I still had about three years of payments left on the loan. I ended up using the money from selling the car to pay off some of the debt on the credit cards that were bursting out of my otherwise empty wallet.

I kept about £500 and I bought a pushbike. I started riding everywhere (in truth, I didn't have a whole lot of choice, since I couldn't afford the car). I used to ride around Peterborough putting little printed flyers I'd made through the letterboxes of all the expensive houses to try to get commissions for my art.

There was this one house I would ride past every day, on arguably the best street in the city. It's a beautiful three-storey house with a basement. It looks regal and there's a beautiful long drive, with room for several cars. There's even a flagpole. It's Victorian, built about 1880, and it stands proud, as close to town as you can get for a house of such size and stature.

Every day I would stop on the path outside that house for ten seconds and just stand there with my bike looking at it. I would repeat to myself, 'One day I'm going to have that house.' At the time, I was single and I didn't have kids – I really didn't have the need for a house like that. It's grand, but it's not the biggest house in the city, that's not why it caught my attention. It just seemed to be talking to me for some reason. It somehow had the balance of everything I'd ever wanted in a dream house.

Fast-forward several years and I'd pivoted from art into property. Mark and I had built a successful property company and portfolio, and I was making some decent money. I still loved that street and that house, and I could finally afford to live there. I had also met and married my wife in the meantime, and she loved the idea of living on that street, too.

But it was 2009, and we were in the middle of the recession. I decided against buying a house at that point, because I predicted that prices might drop further. I thought renting for a year and watching the market would be a better strategy (I'm not necessarily advising this, it's just the approach I decided to take at the time). That way, if prices were to come down even further, I would already be there, so I'd be able to see the 'For Sale' signs pop up and jump on an opportunity.

So we rented a five-bedroom house and planned to live there for maybe six to 12 months. We ended up living there for three years. Bobby was born while we were living in that house, and we had many great times there. Life got busy and exciting, and I kind of forgot about the grand house I used to stop and look at as I rode past on my bike every day.

Being me, I eventually started getting itchy feet and feeling the need to buy something on the street – I love to own property (funny, that!) so renting could only ever be short term for me. I kept my eyes peeled for those 'For Sale' signs, hoping the right one would appear. It did, but not in the way I'd expected.

One day I was getting a haircut. My hairdresser, Anthony James, had been cutting my hair for years in exchange for me giving him business coaching. We'd built a great relationship – we gave each other value – and it turned into a friendship, so we'd chat about all sorts of stuff. In between snips, he said, 'My dad's selling his house.'

He had no idea at the time what that bit of news meant to me. I happened to know it was that house I'd spent ten seconds every day parked outside on my bike. That house I'd visualized owning. That grand Victorian house with a flagpole and enough space for all the cars I wanted ...

'Is it number X?' I asked, pretty sure of the answer already. 'Yeah, that's the one,' he said. I immediately told him I wanted to buy it. I didn't think twice – I had the money in the bank and I wanted to buy it. Anthony went to see his dad at the house and started the ball rolling. I didn't even consider negotiating, I offered the asking price, which was fair. And because we weren't dealing through estate agents, we had no fees to worry about.

I bought the house, and both owners – Anthony's dad and his dad's wife – said they were really happy that they were selling their house to someone they knew, someone who was local and successful in Peterborough.

We all came out of the deal with a positive feeling. We all won. We did a quite a big refurb on the house when we moved in, re-arranging the layout. The previous owners came to visit a couple of years later and commented how much they thought we'd really improved the house, and said they were really pleased and proud that they had sold it to me.

We still live in that dream house today – I could very happily live there for the rest of my life, although my wife wants to build a massive house out in the country ... we'll see how that one plays out.

Luck ... or something else?

We all want to be fortunate. We want good things to happen to us. Of course we do – no one wishes for bad fortune, negative effects, bad luck (apart from the masochists among us ... you know who you are). But the idea of luck and good fortune is more widespread than you might think. In surveys, more than half of people have admitted to being superstitious, and more than 70 per cent have admitted to owning a good luck charm. (Is that a rabbit's foot in your pocket ...?)

Maybe they help, somehow, by making people hopeful. Maybe they do have a function (although, interestingly, one experiment showed that not only did people not feel luckier with a lucky charm, some even felt more unlucky). Personally, I don't go in for this idea of luck being random; I think we have much more control over it.

Now, you could say that buying that house was serendipitous, you could call it luck. By the Oxford English Dictionary's definition, luck is 'success or failure apparently brought by chance rather than through one's own actions'. And, sure, that's one way of looking at it. I was in the right place at the right time. It was by chance that my hairdresser mentioned the sale, by chance that it happened to be my dream house.

But if you break it down, it doesn't seem all that lucky. In fact, it almost seems planned … maybe with a sprinkle of serendipity:

- I took action to tackle my rising debt by selling my car and buying a bike.
- I took action to get art commissions by posting flyers through letterboxes.
- I visualized owning my dream house.
- I pivoted to property and put everything I am into building a successful business.
- I took action and rented a house in the area I liked.
- I created fair exchange of value and built a good relationship with my hairdresser.
- I listened.
- I applied the information I had and spotted an opportunity.
- I made a fast decision.
- I took the opportunity.

If you look through the steps, you can see a series of actions that led to what looked like a lucky outcome. A series of decisions I made to take opportunities that carried me up the driveway and straight into my dream house.

I believe in the serendipity of creating your own luck – creating your own opportunity. I believe luck doesn't just happen; it's a way of describing a favourable outcome that results from a whole string of things you did to set up a situation.

It's a chicken-and-egg situation: are you lucky to have an opportunity, or does the opportunity make you lucky? I believe the latter: luck is good fortune; it's what you enjoy when you grab the right opportunity at the right moment. And I believe you can create your own luck – even if you don't know it at the time. The Israeli business guru Eliyahu M. Goldratt believed something similar: 'Good luck is when opportunity meets preparation,' he said, 'while bad luck is when lack of preparation meets reality.'

Some people use the word 'luck' negatively, almost as an insult. I can't count the number of times someone has put my success down to luck, or accusingly called me 'lucky'. It so often comes with a side of resentment or bitterness, an accusation that the success isn't deserved.

You don't have to take my word for all this – scientists have studied luck and concluded exactly the same thing. According to the Stanford psychologist Alfred Bandura, 'Some of the most important determinants of life paths often arise through the most trivial of circumstances.' These chance encounters, coincidences, right-place-at-the-right-time moments, lucky incidents, are important. But do they just happen? Apparently not.

Professor Richard Wiseman from the University of Hertfordshire is fascinated by luck – why some people seem luckier and what contributes to luck. In fact, he has written a whole book about it, *The Luck Factor* (2003). Over the course of a decade, he studied 400 people, doing experiments with them, asking them to fill in questionnaires and keep diaries, and following their lives. Some of them claimed to be lucky, others unlucky. One even said she was so unlucky that she refused to wish anyone else luck in case she somehow cursed them.

What Wiseman found was far from magic, and definitely not random: 'Although lucky and unlucky people have almost no insight into the real causes of their good and bad luck,' he wrote, 'their thoughts and behaviour are responsible for much of their fortune.' He outlined four main contributors, or principles, to people's perceived luck – and they're all factors we'll cover later in this book, as we explore how to create, spot and seize opportunities:

- The *first principle* is being skilled at creating and noticing chance opportunities. Wiseman showed this really clearly with an experiment using a newspaper. He asked people to tell him how many photos were in the paper; the unlucky people took several minutes, while the lucky ones took only seconds. The difference was down to something the lucky people happened to notice: a message telling them 'Stop counting – there are 43 photographs in this newspaper.'
- The *second principle* is making 'lucky' decisions by listening to their intuition – that gut instinct that's so helpful for taking opportunities that require fast decisions (we'll come back to this in Part 2).
- The *third principle* is creating self-fulfilling prophecies through positive expectations. Let's think back to visualization for a moment. Visualizing your best self was shown to result in more positive expectations, and Wiseman found a link between those expectations and self-fulfilling prophecies: what you visualize becomes reality (or, rather, you make it reality).
- The *fourth principle* is huge, and it's something a lot of people referred to when I asked them what opportunity meant: lucky people tend to adopt a resilient attitude that transforms bad luck into good.

Bad luck as opportunity

Like the people in Wiseman's research, a lot of people think that they have really bad luck, or that other people are just born lucky. They have that simple belief that 'I'm unlucky'. They ask themselves, 'Why does it always happen to me?' and 'Why are other people so lucky?' They complain that 'life isn't fair'. They see themselves as victims of misfortune and think they're helpless to do anything about it – or maybe use that as an excuse to do nothing.

That belief is probably one of the biggest blocks to the flow of opportunity coming to you. Having a victim mindset, believing that everything happens *to* you, will block you from creating and spotting opportunities. You'll end up exacerbating your 'bad luck' and spiralling downwards.

There's another way to see things, and it's reflected in the stories of countless people who have turned their lives around. This is something I've talked to peak performance expert and entrepreneur Ed Mylett about on my podcast. People with this mindset believe that things happen *for* you, not *to* you.

Think of the power of that. If you think things happen *to* you, you're a victim, you're out of control, you're effect rather than causation. You have no ability to change the outcome of your situation; you perceive only the downside and not the upside. But if you always believe things happen *for* you, even the challenges, the hardships, the deepest low points, you realize they're a service to you, rather than an obstacle to you. You believe that everything is given to you to help you prepare for the next level. You perceive an upside in everything. All of a sudden, you can see the opportunity. Nothing has changed, the situation might still be dreadful, but your perception has shifted. You're no longer blind to possibility.

Without knowing her story, you might think that Oprah Winfrey is lucky. With an estimated net worth of over $4 billion, she was the first black woman entrepreneur to make it onto the Bloomberg Billionaires Index. But that success, that so-called 'luck', came after years of hardship.

Growing up in poverty, she was eight when her mother walked out on her. A year later, aged nine, she was raped. She ran away from home to escape sexual abuse and became pregnant at 14; her son died shortly after being born prematurely. When she was sent to live with her father, Oprah took his strict approach and focus on education as an opportunity – she became an honours student and excelled at school, tapping into the encouragement she'd had from her grandmother.

Her media career began in the mid-1970s, when she became the youngest news anchor and the first black female news anchor at WLAC-TV in Nashville. She was fired from her first major job, but that setback didn't stop her from taking herself from poverty and abuse to being the queen of media and the wealthiest African American of the 20th century.

Oprah is a great example that it's possible to change your 'luck'. Seeing negative situations as opportunities is something entrepreneurs have got down to a fine art, but this skill isn't limited to business – it's something you can apply in any aspect of your life. There's nothing stopping you turning your pain into your gain or your strife into a better life. And you can use your own experience to help other people do the same.

Going back to Wiseman's 400 lucky and unlucky research subjects, he wanted to know whether it's possible to change your fortune. In his 'Luck School' he taught people to act more like lucky people do – and 80 per cent of the people who took part said their luck had increased.

The first thing they did was to maximize their opportunities. And that's exactly what we're going to do in the next part of this book.

Summary

Does luck bring opportunity, or does opportunity lead to luck? People can lean on luck as an excuse or an accusation, or blame bad luck for the negative things that happen to them. But there are four principles behind luck, and it's possible to turn around your fortune by learning to apply them.

TAKE ACTION

· ·

How well prepared are you to be lucky?

Score yourself out of ten for these four skills:

1 Creating and noticing chance opportunities ☐
2 Listening to your intuition ☐
3 Visualizing and realizing a positive future ☐
4 Adopting a resilient attitude ☐

What could you do to lift your score in any of these areas?

PART 2

How to prepare for opportunities

5
Get ready

'If you apply yourself to study you will avoid all boredom with
life, you will not long for night because you are sick of daylight,
you will be neither a burden to yourself nor useless to others, you
will attract many to become your friends and the finest people
will flock about you.'

Seneca, 'On the Shortness of Life'

By now you should be able to see that we're surrounded by opportunities at every turn, and that they're all there for the taking. You've
also started working on your own opportunities. You've defined
what opportunity means to you, you have thought about what you'd
do if you only had a year to live, you've scanned your life for opportunities you're not taking (yet), you've done a bit of visualization,
and you've scored yourself on the four skills you need to be 'lucky'.

Great work – pat yourself on the back! Now I've lulled you
into thinking that's as hard as it gets, I'm going to drop you in
at the deep end. Grab yourself a coffee (mine's a medium skinny
cappuccino with an extra shot, thanks) and get ready to work.
Because this section is all about self-development. It's about learning and adapting and changing your behaviour, your thoughts,
your reactions, your assumptions. It's about figuring out what
you're doing – and not doing – to seize opportunities, adjust your
life and start winning.

This is the painful bit. Self-development is all about getting
uncomfortable, embracing change and recognizing and adapting
to new ways of doing things. Basically, all the stuff you want to
avoid with every fibre of your being.

My self-development journey over the last 15 years has been transformational, but make no mistake, it's also been f★★★ing hard. Do I really have to make that call, ignore that troll, try that new thing? Why can't I just sit in front of the telly with one hand holding a beer and the other one down my pants? I'm kidding (I don't drink), but there's an important point here.

It's human nature to avoid change, to avoid doing something differently or to avoid spending time and energy learning something new. We're all cavepeople at heart, and we're busy surviving by doing the same things day in day out. Even if most of us have swapped our clubs for iPhones.

Change might be unpleasant or even scary, but I believe that even the caveman/woman in you can learn to create, spot, assess and take opportunities.

Academics say that these are skills you can learn; opportunity identification is becoming a big part of education around business and entrepreneurship. Experts in this field treat it as a competency, like communication or decision making or leadership. Experiments have shown that students can identify more opportunities, have more and better and more innovative ideas, just by learning the skill and process behind identifying opportunities.

In short, you might not be a natural when it comes to opportunity identification, but even if you're a disaster, you can learn to be a master. In this part of the book, I'm going to share everything I know about how to prepare.

I think there are four steps in the opportunity process:

1 *Create the conditions* – first, you make changes to your mindset, behaviour and environment.
2 *Spot the opportunity* – second, you notice the opportunity.
3 *Assess the opportunity* – third, you look at the opportunity critically and make some decisions about it.
4 *Take the opportunity* – fourth, you seize the opportunity – or not.

We've gone through the theory in Part 1, this is where we get more practical. You've learned the rules of the road, now it's time to get behind the wheel. (Don't worry, you can trust me, I don't crash supercars every day.) In Part 2, we're focusing on how to prepare for opportunity. In Part 3, we'll look at what to do when opportunity appears.

A couple of thousand years ago, the Roman philosopher Seneca wrote the quote I've included at the start of this chapter. He was a Stoic and he believed that we can be better people by constantly learning and developing ourselves. He thought this made us more useful to ourselves and to society and that, as a result, good people will want to be around us. I agree with him. Seneca and the other Stoics were real gluttons for punishment at times – they lived up to their values, which meant suffering in order to be and do good.

Today, we describe people as 'stoic' if they go through hard times without complaining, suffer without whining. We all know that person who's faced some kind of hardship like cancer or unemployment or a house fire and worked through the experience with grace, seemingly taking it in their stride. And wow, it can really make you feel shit about how much you moan over the small things, can't it?

I think it's good to remember this feeling. To know that you really haven't got it so bad. We're all living in our own contexts, with our own experiences and problems and feelings. But there is always someone who's got it worse than you, and who's complaining less than you are.

Being stoic by taking a Stoic philosophy approach means learning – gathering knowledge, learning new skills and being the best you can be, even if it's hard. You've got to have guts and grit and get-up-and-go to really make changes if you want to seize opportunities and win at life. I think the secret to seizing opportunities is having the right mindset. Years ago, my public speaking coach used to say, 'The skillset without the mindset will leave you upset.'

Mindset is a term that gets bandied around all the time, and a lot of that stuff drives me mad because it can be really hollow. For a long time, I resisted writing my own book on the topic, *I'm Worth More*, because of that – I didn't want it to be just another load of hot air to add to the mix. What I ended up writing was a book about the mindset that separates the really successful people across all areas of life and business – sport, politics, art, entrepreneurship – from everyone else. I discovered that they need to have a mental attitude that's focused, flexible and determined.

There is a lot to say about attitude and mindset, and I'll get into some of it in the next few chapters. For now, I'll just say: put on your determined face, whatever that looks like, and get ready to make changes.

Create the conditions

You'll only be able to seize opportunities if you make it possible for them to happen. I don't just mean by creating opportunities, but also by setting the stage for them – by getting yourself and your environment ready.

Expecting opportunities to just appear before you is like expecting a bird to nest on your wall without putting out a box. Or expecting to win the lottery without buying a ticket. Or expecting a tree to grow if you haven't even planted the seed.

In 1854, the great French biologist Louis Pasteur wrote, 'Dans les champs de l'observation le hasard ne favorise que les esprits préparés' (yeah, I can't read that either. It means: 'In the fields of observation chance favours only the prepared minds'). Generations of people have been repeating these words ever since Pasteur first used them, because they apply much more broadly than to just experimental science.

I think it's a concept that we all seem to know instinctively. Let's look again at what people said when I asked my network about opportunity. Many people said something along the lines of the Pasteur quote, that opportunity is something that happens when you're ready for it.

They are among good people – google 'opportunity' and 'preparation' and you'll get a whole load of advice and wisdom from people throughout history. The actor Milton Berle, the racing driver Bobby Unser and US president Abraham Lincoln are all credited with snappy soundbites saying the same thing: 'opportunity and preparation are linked. If you want to win at life, you need to prepare for opportunity.'

'If opportunity doesn't knock, build a door.'

Milton Berle

'Success is where preparation and opportunity meet.'

Bobby Unser

'I will prepare and someday my chance will come.'

Abraham Lincoln

There are a lot of ways to prepare for opportunity, to create the conditions in which you can make opportunities appear, invite them in or let them develop. We're going to run through the biggest ones here:

- Get to know yourself.
- Put yourself out there (more).
- Find the balance.
- Fill your brain …
- … And now empty your brain.
- Step outside your comfort zone.
- Use your mistakes.

We'll look at each of these in the following chapters.
Ready? Let's make some opportunities happen.

Summary

So, I'm hoping by now that you've started looking more closely at your own life to spot areas you can improve on in order to seize more opportunities and win at life. In the following chapters we're rolling up our sleeves and getting more practical. You're going to develop yourself in order to create the conditions for opportunity to happen. It's not easy to change, but with the right mindset and a good strong coffee, you'll soon be on your way.

TAKE ACTION
• •
Is your head in the right place?

Before you turn the page, take a moment to think about the things you've complained about recently. Look back at the last week (if you're pretty stoic) or the last hour (if you're a master moaner) and write your complaints in a list. How many of the things on the list can you do something about? How many things are you blaming other people for, but which were actually caused or exacerbated by your own inaction? Choose one you can take action on and decide what you're going to do. If it takes 15 minutes or less, do it now. If it takes longer, put it on your list for later. Now you've sparked your active mindset.

6

Get to know yourself

Who are you?

Who are you *really*?

Do you know? Have you invested in not only developing yourself but actually knowing who you are?

I've spent 15 years working really hard on my personal development. I've invested huge amounts of time and money – well over a million pounds – on learning and developing my skills and mindset.

For about the first decade, I was applying what I'd learned to teaching people about property – my first area of expertise. Over the last five years or so, that focus has broadened to cover business, entrepreneurship and, more recently, life in general. I've done hundreds, probably thousands, of videos, including Facebook Lives.

I'm an over-sharer. I share what I'm doing, my struggles and challenges, my pain, my successes and failures, my good days and bad days, my frustrations and moans, and trolls and triumphs. I like to keep it relevant and valuable – I draw the line at telling you about what socks I've chosen or what I'm having for breakfast, although if your luck's in you might get a glimpse of my manly chest (much to my wife's disapproval).

When I started sharing more personal content on social media, about the struggles we all experience in day-to-day life and business, I got a huge reaction – more people started watching and commenting; they really wanted more of *me* – the raw, unedited me.

In therapy

In 2019, I massively upped my content game. I turned 40 at the start of the year, and I set a goal to make it my biggest year ever. I'd been inspired watching an extremely moving documentary film about Alexander McQueen* – in fact, I'd say it was life changing for me. McQueen had struggled with mental health issues and tragically committed suicide by hanging himself in 2010, at the age of 40.

It was a big wake-up call for me. I had always admired McQueen for his amazing designs. I've seen close-up what mental health problems can do to a family. I was going to be the age McQueen was when he died, and it made me realize it was time to really do something, to really start to seize every opportunity.

I wanted to help more people, get more followers and make more money than I ever had before.

I launched new mastermind groups, courses and programmes, and I put myself out there on social media in a big way. I shared even more than I used to, and people responded. They loved the content, they loved my oversharing and they started sharing with me, too.

It ended up being a huge year for me and my businesses – I hit my goal and then some. But it wasn't always easy or even fun. At times it was completely draining. I felt exhausted and lonely. I didn't have the support I needed. I questioned whether it was worth it.

Don't get me wrong, I'm not blaming anyone – I went into it with my eyes open and I take full responsibility. But I felt alone, even when people were around.

It was my biggest year and it was my hardest year. So I hired a therapist.

It wasn't something I'd planned, but I felt like therapy was the one thing I hadn't tried on my self-development journey. And after just a few sessions I realized it was absolutely transformational. I learned more about myself in just a few months of therapy than I had in 15 years of personal development with coaches and mentors.

McQueen (2018), directed by Ian Bonhôte and Peter Ettedgui.

One of the things I've noticed is that, by knowing myself better, I'm better prepared for opportunity. I can see when I'm sticking my head in the sand, or doing something to please someone else rather than for myself, or holding back out of fear, or avoiding judgement or rejection. Seeing it means I can change my behaviour and be more open to opportunity.

I started sharing some of the things I'd covered in my therapy sessions, and the deeper I went, the more people responded. Could it be voyeurism? Maybe. We all like to know people's innermost secrets, especially if those secrets make us feel better. But I think it's more to do with seeing that we're all the same inside – we're all hurt and scared, we all carry baggage from our childhoods, we all struggle in our own way.

I don't just share for the followers or the engagement or the love (although you might get a bit more than you bargained for if you shoot me some Facebook Stars!). My hope is that by sharing my own journey in this kind of detail, other people will start to think about themselves differently and more deeply.

The more I explore, the more open I become. The pain I had hidden from in my past had been holding me back, and now that I'm finally shining some light on it (literally in some cases, like my fear of the dark – which I'm still working on a bit, if I'm honest), it's releasing me. I'm more open to sharing, to being honest, to talking about things that I used to find embarrassing or shameful.

It's also helping me accept and even love a lot of the things about myself that I'd shut away. And I'm sharing mine to make it OK for you to be OK with yours.

I'm a total therapy evangelist now, and I don't think it's only for people who have 'problems' or are 'broken'. But I know not everyone will be up for it. I think there's still a bit of stigma around therapy, certainly in the UK, and I hope that disappears so that more people will feel comfortable talking about their own lives.

Why am I talking about therapy? I think self-awareness is really fundamental to creating the conditions to seize opportunities.

Nurturing self-awareness

This self-awareness works at different levels. At the top level, understanding yourself – including everything that's hiding in the shady corners and cobwebby closets – will help you catch your own self-destructive behaviour, your own actions that are holding back opportunities. You can only change what you see, and self-awareness is about truly seeing yourself.

You can do this quite mechanically – you don't need a couch and a box of tissues (I'm talking about therapy – get your head out of the gutter).

There are loads of ways to build self-awareness by tracking your activities. Some people track their activities over the course of a few weeks and then analyse them to find out what works well, what they could change and what they need to ditch. (I've got a version of this that I explain in my book in 'Routine = Results', the appendix to my book *Start Now, Get Perfect Later*. I'll outline it in detail in Part 5.)

You might want to record the tasks you work on throughout the day and how long they take or how successful they are. You might want to track your sleep or your eating habits or your exercise. You might think about analysing your meetings or events or even your dates. You could track your energy levels, your mood, your physical or mental strength, the length of your wick (because we all have a temper sometimes), or when you feel excited.

Knowledge about any and all of these things will help you understand yourself better. You might discover that you're the kind of person who's best following one task with clear focus or clarity, which could mean you're better off taking one opportunity decisively and following it through to the end. Or maybe you're the kind of person who needs variety and excitement, and would function better by taking several opportunities and seizing them in bitesize chunks.

Knowing how you work, how you function, how you *live*, means you're better prepared for opportunity. And as our old pal Pasteur said, it's all about preparation.

It's not just about the logistics, though. By understanding your-self at a deeper level, you can start to see what is – and isn't – an opportunity that's right for you. Knowing yourself is the foun-dation of all the other steps to seizing opportunities. You need to know yourself in order to spot what's right for you, assess each opportunity according to your life, habits and values, and take the right opportunities at the right times.

I've talked about my life as a skint artist, that I couldn't, or didn't, see the opportunities that were right in front of me. One of the big reasons for this was that I didn't really know myself back then. I was young and naïve, and sure, I was gorgeous and irresist-ible to women (I wished!), but it was all a front. My dark artistic side was just masking the person I really was – the one who was hidden away because of my own fear.

Before my journey of self-development and discovery started, I was blind to myself. It seems ridiculous, but it's true. I see this every day, because the more I get to know myself, first through self-development and now through therapy, the more opportuni-ties appear in my life.

Choosing who you are

As much as it's a process of discovery – of finding and under-standing who you really are – it's also a process of invention. I chose to be that struggling artist, and when my life changed the day my dad had his big breakdown, I chose to change. I chose to go to a networking meeting, and I chose to be the person who talked to total strangers and build new relationships. I chose to learn and develop and grow. I chose to be the person I needed to be in order to achieve what I wanted to.

Fabienne Fredrickson, the founder of Boldheart (formerly the Client Attraction Business School), says that being is the first step to success. She believes you don't achieve your goals – such as creating opportunities – by just doing things, you also have to be something. She says you first have to look at what you want, your end goal, and then work out who you need to be in order to achieve that goal. Then comes the doing. And then comes having – you get what you want.

I think she's right. There's a lot of advice kicking around about being 'authentic' and 'staying true to yourself', and I think there's some truth in that. But who we are isn't fixed – we can change. We can learn and develop and grow. We can break bad habits and begin good ones. We can overcome our fears and be more confident. All these things change who we are, to a certain extent.

The US entrepreneur Ed Mylett takes this idea a step further. If you don't know Ed, google him and watch a few videos. Better yet, listen to my interview with him on my podcast *The Disruptive Entrepreneur* (it's one of my favourite episodes, and you'll see why – he got some massive news right before we recorded and not only did he go ahead with the interview, but he also shared the news and was open about it. What a guy!). He's high-energy; he makes me look stoned – and that's saying something!

Mylett's view is that you can't always control external factors. But it doesn't matter – they don't control the direction of your life. It's what's inside – your identity – that controls everything. He likens your identity to a personal thermostat. It works just like a room with heating, where the thermostat controls the room's temperature regardless of whether it's snowing or sunny outside.

And let's face it, sometimes it is snowing outside. Or hailing. Or there's a tornado. Sometimes things go wrong – you feel like you've worked yourself into the ground but you're not getting that break. You've tried everything but you're not meeting your one true love. You're trying to lose weight, but you just don't have the time …

The thermostat Mylett talks about is what I talk about in my book *I'm Worth More* – it's mindset. What I like about the analogy is that it shows how adjustable our identities can be. We can tweak them however we need to in order to reach our goals.

But before you can change, you need to know yourself. You need to know what you're dealing with. I could only make the changes I needed to by really looking at myself and saying 'Rob, you're creative but you don't need to be a struggling artist, you can be creative in business. You're disruptive but you don't need to be poor. You're a fixer but you don't have to pander to other people.'

Now there's one huge caveat to this: I don't think you ever need to change your core, your essence, who you really are deep down. There are certain things about me that I know are here to stay. I'm working on the law of least effort, but I'm impatient and impetuous; I'd rather try a bit too hard and push people away and maybe piss a few people off. Will that change? No. One bloke hated the audio version of my book *Money* because of my accent, but I've never even considered doing elocution lessons. Will that change? No. (You can take the man out of Peterborough …)

The great thing about investing your time, effort and money in knowing yourself is that you'll get to know the parts of you that are permanent and unmovable and the parts that you can change, shift, adapt and develop. By understanding who you are, you'll see who you could be. You'll start to use your unique set of skills, experiences and traits to add value to other people.

Know yourself and you'll be prepared for the opportunities that are right for you.

Summary

By getting to know yourself, you will be better prepared for opportunity when it knocks. Personal development and therapy have helped me understand myself better, and it's constantly opening new opportunities. Some parts of you are fixed, but you can change yourself, your identity, to help you achieve whatever goal you set for yourself.

TAKE ACTION
· ·
Who are you?

1 On a blank page, write down three words to describe yourself. Now underneath that write down three words that other people would use to describe you. Do they match? Why? Doing this will give you an idea of how well you know yourself and how open you are with others. If you want to explore this more deeply, you could ask people to describe you in a few words, then use that as a starting point for a conversation.

2 Now list five things you value most. Do they connect to the words you used to describe yourself? Or the words other people would use? Do you feel that you're living to your values? Are there any changes you could make to better align to them?

3 Write down three things you fear. Are you taking responsibility for overcoming these things? Are you controlling your thermostat? If not, what could you do to take control?

4 Now write down three things you want. Is the person you described at the start the person who will achieve those three things? If not, what do you need to change to make it happen? Write down at least one way you could change, develop or grow to achieve your goals. Remember, you don't have to be someone different, but you do have the power to choose your identity.

7
Put yourself out there (more)

I've already talked a bit about my oversharing, but I have loads more to say, so sit tight.

I'm kind of half joking here, because actually, having a lot to say about, well, pretty much anything and everything is what really helped open doors for me.

I want to take you back to the night I went to my first property networking meeting. I showed up, new kid on the block, jazzy shirt, full of energy and not much else, and started talking. I've always had the gift of the gab. Maybe it was being raised in a pub that did it, but I'm certainly not lost for words too often. Even back then when I was scared and clueless, I still managed to talk people's ears off.

You know how cats seem to gravitate towards the people who hate cats? Well, that night I was a cat, a very talkative cat, and Mark was the infinitely less talkative cat disliker. (That's unfair of me – Mark does like cats.) I bowled up to him at that networking event and started talking. I talked and talked, and 15 years later he's my partner in several businesses.

Networking is the stuff of nightmares for a lot of people. The thought of walking into a room of people and talking to total strangers can be enough to kick-start a heart attack. I hated the idea at first, but I knew I had to get over that fear and do it anyway if I wanted those (literal) doors to open.

When I was working in my first property job, there was an opportunity to speak at an event. I jumped in and volunteered before anyone had a chance to say a word. I went on a public speaking course, and in the last 15 years I've earned two world records and made millions of pounds speaking at events all over the world.

You think networking is bad? Ask people about public speaking – it ranks *above death* as the world's number-one phobia. People would rather die than get up on stage! Don't get me wrong, I didn't love the idea at first, but I knew I had to get over my fear if I wanted to take new opportunities that would propel my career.

I didn't just go from sitting in my room above my parents' pub, listening to metal music, making art and being poor and miserable, to walking out on stage and talking for 48 straight hours to break a world record. That's not how these things go. That would have killed me.

It's about getting *progressively* uncomfortable, not *aggressively* uncomfortable. You need to layer your exposure to failure. If you try to go from one to a hundred in a split second, you're setting yourself up for a shock; do it gradually and you're much more likely to succeed.

Make no mistake, it will be uncomfortable. Personal development is uncomfortable. I'm sure you've heard a million people over the years saying you have to 'get out of your comfort zone'. I don't think that's always the right advice – sometimes you need to listen to that gut feeling that says STOP! – but, in general, I think that being uncomfortable means you're pushing yourself, stretching your abilities, testing your boundaries, and that's how you make change and invite opportunities.

Get visible

Putting yourself out there is probably the most important thing you can do to create the conditions to invite opportunities, seize the day and win at life. In fact, if you only do one thing in this whole book, make it this one. I bet you didn't want to read that;

this is the thing that takes the most effort and energy and action. But it's worth it. So just f★★★ing do it.

It's not elegant, it's not refined, it's not complicated. It's simple. It's attritional. Everyone can do it. It doesn't have to be perfect (nothing does – I'll take you through my 'start now, get perfect later' approach in Part 5) so you can get moving and improve as you go.

All you have to do is *put yourself out there more.*

Way more.

I see it again and again in the people I mentor. They have great products and services but they're not where they want to be. The first thing I tell them is to get out there; be everywhere.

Remember how strange it felt to enter a state of lockdown in the spring of 2020, when the coronavirus pandemic seismically transformed the way we lived and interacted with each other? Being told to stay at home to stay safe made sense, but people around the world soon discovered that, among the many drawbacks of isolation, there was a feeling of pulling back from the world, of becoming invisible. So we began reaching out in other ways – conversations over the garden fence, Zoom calls with friends we'd almost lost touch with, starting a podcast or getting involved with our community. Being seen and interacting with others is tremendously important. It's the same in business.

There's a saying: visibility is credibility. Nothing exists in a vacuum. You can have the best product or service in the world, but if no one sees it, it doesn't exist. You could be the best singer in the world, but if your music doesn't land on the ears of millions of people, it doesn't exist. You could be a public speaker, but if you're on stage in a dark, empty room, you are not a public speaker.

You need to be way more visible.

Part of my big 40 plans for 2019, to celebrate my 40th birthday, was a huge increase in content: more podcasts, more videos, more live events, more masterclasses and mentoring programmes, more 'ask me anything' posts, more calls, more interviews, more articles, more books, more sharing. More everything.

It was exhausting, but it worked – 2019 was the biggest year of my life.

Putting myself out there has set off many chain reactions in all different directions, creating the conditions for opportunities all over the place. Take my podcast, *The Disruptive Entrepreneur*. I had an amazing guest on, Maisie Williams. She is an award-winning actor who played Arya Stark on *Game of Thrones* (I assume this means something to you … if not, what rock have you been living under?). She's a huge star, and I really wasn't expecting to get her on as a guest.

Here's where putting myself out there opened up an opportunity: her communications guy had read some of my books, including *Money*. I put myself out there with that book – it was the result of ten years of research into money, 155,000 words written in blood, sweat and tears (not to mention all the rewriting and editing) and relentless marketing. Some random, amazing people have read that book, including Maisie Williams's comms guy.

I put myself out there big time, and an opportunity appeared. That wouldn't have happened if I'd kept all that knowledge to myself. It wouldn't have happened without me writing the book, publishing it and marketing it.

You never know who's out there reading your book, listening to your podcast, consuming your content. If you're putting yourself out there, you'll be connecting with a lot of people without even realizing it.

The goal is to be more visible in order to widen your network. You can do that at live networking events, like the one where I talked Mark's ears off. But to make that an effective strategy, you can't talk to the same old people, the faces that you see every month. Go to new events, charity balls, panel discussions, speed networking sessions. Every new person you connect with has their own network of people; you grow your network exponentially by meeting new people. And in no time you'll be one move away from Kevin Bacon.

Seek the uncomfortable feeling of introducing yourself to someone new, unfamiliar, potentially important. That's the same uncomfortable feeling you get when you go live on Facebook, or publish a blog post, or post a YouTube video, or get on stage. It's that same fight-or-flight hormone response we looked at in Chapter 1 – the one you need to harness and turn into excitement.

Go for it

Let's come back to that saying, visibility is credibility. Back in 2001, the newspapers in the UK ran a lead photo story about a team shot of Manchester United. It's a shot that you see all the time, but what made this one special was that it featured a new face – someone who wasn't actually in the team.

Karl Power was a huge Man United fan (each to their own, we can't all have good taste) and wanted to pull a prank that would get him close to the team. Karl and his friend Tommy Dunn, who are now gate-crashing legends, hatched a plan in the Old Nag's Head, a pub that's around the corner from Man United's home ground, Old Trafford. They decided they would pose as journalists at a match in Munich, and then, just at the right moment, Karl would run onto the pitch and join the team for their photo.

'When you show a bit of authority, no one questions that,' Tommy said in a BBC interview in 2016. The plan worked – Tommy gave Karl the signal and he stripped off his tracksuit to reveal a full away kit, matching the team.

'As I walked to that line-up, the adrenaline rush was just unbelievable,' Karl told the BBC.

He used that adrenaline, he turned it into excitement and stood there with the world's (then) most famous football team, and nobody, not even the players (well, all except one), noticed. It took one sharp-eyed photographer to raise the flag, and the next day Karl was world famous.

The two friends have since organized all sorts of mad pranks: Karl has run on to bat at an England cricket match, appeared on the podium at the Formula One British Grand Prix, played a few volleys at Wimbledon, recreated a legendary goal just a few minutes before kick-off at Old Trafford and sneaked into the 2014 World Cup final.

OK, so they've been banned from Old Trafford and they haven't made many friends in the sporting world, but they've appeared on TV and basically turned themselves into expert gate-crashers.

I'm not suggesting you cook up any elaborate pranks, but there's a lot to learn from these two mad blokes. The biggest thing, I think, is something Tommy said in an interview with *Business Insider*: 'Go for it. Otherwise, what's the point?'

This is where confidence comes in. You need to believe in yourself and overcome the fear of putting yourself out there. Once you do, simply being visible means people will see you as credible. There's automatic credibility in being seen, in being noticed. Just think about Karl Power, standing with the Man United team. He seemed credible just because he was there.

Even if you're not the best, even if you've only been doing whatever it is you're doing for a short amount of time, you can still get credibility through visibility.

Get online

This is even truer on social media. Thanks to the algorithms, the more you are seen, the more you are seen; the wider your net, the wider your net.

I think there are loads of ways you can use social media to put yourself out there. Like I said, I'm an oversharer, so you might not be comfortable going as deep as I do. But it's so easy to put yourself out there by documenting what you do in your day, week, life, so the world can see it. I don't mean sharing your address and bank account details and the birthdays of your kids, but taking people 'behind the scenes' in your life can really help open up opportunities for you.

This is absolutely true in business, and that's probably the easiest area of your life to draw lines around. You know your job or expertise or profession, and you can choose to put yourself out there around that. You might want to do blog posts or a podcast or live videos or publish a book showcasing your expertise; the more people that content reaches, the more your network will grow.

I think it also counts for other areas in life. Social media is great for meeting people you might not otherwise bump into (so I hear). You'll only get the opportunity to meet someone on Tinder if you are on Tinder. You'll only connect with your future partner in a *Star Wars* fan club forum if you're posting in that forum. You need to get out there and be you if you want to attract the right opportunities.

To a lot of us 40-plussers, this is all a bit weird. 'Look at me doing this, straightening my hair / putting on my make-up / cleaning my car', and so on. What is it with these video clips of people dancing or lip-syncing or making their lips all puffy or their bum rounder?

But think about your audience. If you're in business and you want to reach young people, this is their life – for a 15-year-old, or even a 25-year-old, there was no life before the internet. It's totally normal for them to live in a *Matrix*-style parallel world where they're living their real lives and documenting it all on Instagram and TikTok. This is the way the world is now. (Actually, I'm testing TikTok … it's a great place for bloopers and weirdness and super-speed tips, though I'm not quite ready to lip sync or dance like a teenager to cheesy pop music.)

OK, you might not want to go as far as mad clips on TikTok, but there's a lot of value in social media. The more you put yourself out there, the more you're boosting your reach, your brand, your exposure, your visibility, your connections, your partnerships, your collaborations, your joint ventures and … drumroll … your opportunities.

Let's say you want to be a public speaker. The speakers who get paid the most are not necessarily the best speakers, they're the most visible ones. Having a million followers on Instagram makes you way more noticeable than giving a few life-changing after-dinner speeches to a hundred people. That speaker with a million followers gets paid way more than the one who's a better speaker but doesn't have a following on social media. I know of billionaires who are getting £20,000 for a speech, while not-quite-millionaires are charging upwards of £100,000.

It might seem unfair that the person who's more skilled is less in demand, but that's life. Life isn't fair. You're not going to be rewarded just for having something to say; you actually have to go out there and say it. I've heard people giving the advice that you should keep opinions to yourself, but I think that's wrong. Everyone has equal right to give their opinion. Sure, plenty of opinions are just noise, but many – including yours – are valuable. You just need to be careful not to say your opinion is fact, or say it with such volition, so loudly, that people think it's the gospel. But sharing your opinions can encourage others to do the same, and that openness means people can learn from each other's experiences.

Sharing your opinion can give you visibility. Visibility is credibility. Visibility means you can increase your fees, do new things, meet more people, grow your network, find partners, and so on, in every area of your life.

Get noticed

Early on my own personal development journey, I did some courses with a trainer who worked with a promotion company that was visible all around the world. This training company was huge, running events for thousands of people. The turnover must have been in the tens of millions of pounds. I took part in most of the courses they offered – a speaking course, a personal development course, 'warrior spirit'-type courses, some money courses – and I became one of their best students.

I always made myself get noticed at the events: I would wear bright stand-out clothing, I would always ask interesting questions if there was a Q&A, and I would always stand up to ask them even if everyone else sat down. I would try to speak to the crew and the team, and even to the main trainer if I could get near them. Pretty soon they started to notice me and talk about me. This was around the time that Mark and I were building up our training companies, and we were getting a little bit of a name and a reputation for ourselves.

Then, almost out of nowhere, the promotion company went into voluntary liquidation. They put together a package to sell the company, which at that point had £800,000 worth of courses outstanding that needed to be delivered. Of course, there were a few people sniffing around – it looked like a great opportunity, despite the liability. But the owner of the promotion company pretty much didn't want to talk to anyone except me. He wanted a buyer that would do the right thing, and I think he saw that in me.

We bought the company for a very small amount of money, with virtually no money down. We took on the responsibility to deliver all the courses. And we delivered all £800,000 worth of courses. We had to move some things around and change trainers, which we were entitled to do, but we got it done. That meant every single one of the people who could have lost the thousands of pounds that they had paid for a course didn't – they got trained by us, and we even gave them extra courses and materials to make them happy.

That company has done tens of millions of pounds since, and it's a company we still run today.

I believe that opportunity came about because I put myself out there, because I was doing the right thing by the company in the first place. I was present, I'd invested in myself through them, I was active, I asked questions and made myself visible. They knew me. By putting myself out there, I had forged a relationship with that company, and this allowed me to recognize and take the opportunity when it came up. (I made the decision fast and furiously – that's one approach to *taking* opportunities.)

This isn't the only example of a business opportunity that's come about by getting visible. In fact, it's not even the only company we've bought. In the early years of Mark and me buying property together, we were trying to manage everything ourselves. We were overstretched and overconfident, and we soon figured out that we weren't good at managing properties – letting agents are good at that, entrepreneurs not so much. It takes a lot of logistics and admin and you need to be seriously organized. Needless to say, we didn't enjoy it much and it was proving to be quite a lot of work for not much pay-off. So we decided to hire a letting agency to manage our properties.

Our usual go-to strategy for finding a good opportunity in the form of a partnership or consultant or provider is to ask people we know, like and trust for recommendations. Mark was having conversations with someone who was a bit more experienced with property than we were back in 2006, and he was getting some good tips and advice from him. He seemed to know what he was talking about, so Mark asked him if he knew a letting agency. He recommended one, and over the next five years they managed more than 350 properties in our personal and clients' portfolios. It was a good partnership.

Then this letting agency got into some trouble, and it looked like they were going to have to either liquidate or sell. We put in a rescue sales bid, and because we had the most properties with them, they favoured our bid above all the others. We ended up buying the letting agency – again, for very good value – and in doing that we brought many of the properties back in house. That was also how our letting agency, Progressive Lets, got a standing start. It now has over 850 lets and is the second largest letting agency in our home city, Peterborough.

These two stories are both to do with visibility. We took over a promotion and training company because I had put myself out there and made connections. We took over a letting agency because Mark had put himself out there and made connections. But added to the visibility was a real focus on developing meaningful relationships. I think what makes the big difference there is listening.

Get listening and asking

Virtually all your opportunities are going to come through people, just like these did for us. As I shared in Chapter 1, I believe opportunity is everywhere, and I think there are opportunities that come with every person we meet. There are loads of reasons we might not even notice them – maybe we're simply not making enough connections or being social enough or networking enough (I hope that, by reading this chapter, you'll pull your finger out and stop it holding you back from your opportunities). But I think a really common issue, the reason why most people are held back from opportunities, is that they don't listen. They have one-way conversations and monologues rather than dialogues. They talk *at* people rather than listen *to* people.

Now you might be thinking, 'Come on, Rob, you're one to talk, you never shut up!' and you're right, I do talk a lot. But actually, I listen even more than I talk. There's a reason we've got two ears and one mouth. (Can you imagine how much I'd talk if I had two mouths?) If I meet someone new, I want to know what I can learn from them, what information or experience or insights they have that I can benefit from. If you just let people talk, it's amazing how much of their life and their experience and their problems they will share with you, even people who you've not met before. Listen to people and they will give you solutions, they will give you advice, they will give you gossip, they will give you insights, they will give you trade secrets.

What's really amazing is that they'll also feel more connected to you than if you'd shared your own life story with them. That's a brilliant way to start a relationship that will open doors for you.

This is something hostage negotiators do. They're under pressure and need to build trust fast with someone who is often dangerous, mentally unstable and even delusional. Chris Voss, a former FBI hostage negotiator and now a business negotiation expert, teaches people how to do this in order to succeed in business negotiations. One of the basic skills he teaches is linked to listening and building trust. It's called mirroring. The idea is that you repeat the last few words of a sentence someone says to you in order to come across as engaged and to encourage them to continue.

Imagine you're at a property networking event and you're talking to a potential investor. Here's how a conversation might go:

INVESTOR: ... And at the moment I've got a portfolio of properties across the UK but mostly in London.

YOU: Mostly in London?

INVESTOR: Yes, I know, it was a bit odd at first since I don't live there, but I had an opportunity I couldn't pass up and it ended up being a huge success.

YOU: A huge success?

INVESTOR: Yeah, we made a much bigger profit than we expected, so I invested in another property ...

You get the picture. It seems a bit weird, but if you try it in a real-life setting, you'll realize it's more natural than it looks in black and white, and doing it actually helps you listen better. Listening is a skill everyone can learn. People generally don't listen to the same degree, and that's down to their own sense of self (and sometimes self-importance).

I believe people don't listen either because they're waiting to talk, because they want to prove themselves, or because they don't believe that they can learn from certain people, so they just dismiss them. I don't think like that. I have a mentality that none of us are above or below anyone else – we are all equal – and therefore we can all learn from everyone.

As well as listening and mirroring, you have to ask very good questions. Asking good questions loosens people's grip on defensiveness, softens their social awkwardness, warms up a cold conversation and gets you into a flow.

So I ask people questions about their lives and their experiences, about their knowledge and their wisdom. I ask them for their advice and opinions, their help and guidance, their mentorship and support. There's nothing bad about asking for help – I ask for help all the time, and that often brings with it opportunities.

Asking people questions and listening shows them that you're interested. It makes people want to talk to you – they feel noticed and heard, and they trust you. That's how you make connections, that's how you get visible, and that's what will get you prepared for opportunity.

Position yourself

In Chapter 6, I asked you to think about who you are, to explore yourself a bit and try to get a deeper understanding of what makes you *you*. When you put yourself out there, you need to be clear about this in order to position yourself.

I'm positioning myself as 'The Disruptive Entrepreneur': someone who teaches start-ups and scale-ups. If you want to make more money, if you want to grow your businesses and your brands and your empires, I'm your man! I'm not just putting myself out there to be seen, but actually to be known in a certain way. It's next-level visibility.

My positioning hasn't always been this broad. These days I talk a lot about entrepreneurship, business and life in general, but before I widened my positioning through podcasting and authorship, for about eight years I positioned myself as a property expert. My book

Life Leverage was my bridge between niche property positioning and more general entrepreneurship. My next level might be general human behaviour and personal development, which includes money and business but also mindset and personal growth.

It's probably wise to go an inch wide and a mile deep at the start – super niche. If you're known for something specific, it's easier for people to find you, connect with you, work with you and partner with you, bringing you more and more opportunities. Then once you get known, you can go a bit shallower and a bit wider.

Of course, the content you share makes a difference, and we haven't really touched on that. I think that's a whole series of books (*makes another note*), so I won't go into detail here. But I do want to say something about the tone of what you put out there.

I'm not a believer in controversy for the sake of it. I think there's a lot of gimmicks out there where people are being very controversial just to get noticed, and to me that's a bit shallow. I think if you do controversial content and make waves just to get noticed, that could backfire on you, as it could be perceived as lacking substance. It might look like you're just attacking people or putting people down or getting involved in controversial debates as a way to get exposure.

That doesn't mean I'm against making waves. I'm the Disruptive Entrepreneur, after all. But what's the context and the meaning and the purpose of the content? If you can make waves that are relevant, on concept with your brand and your message and how you want to be known, and valuable to your audience, I think that will make a huge difference to you.

For example, you might be brutally honest in order to attract relationship opportunities and find the right person. You might want to start a movement and get people fired up about something. Or maybe you're looking to set yourself apart in business by appealing to a specific target group.

My brand is called Disruptive. If you see or hear me speak in public, I'm very disruptive. I hit the audience hard, I polarize the audience, I'm quite outspoken at times and I can have the audience in fits of laughter.

And I have clothes that get noticed. That might not be the first thing you consider when you're planning to put yourself out there more but, believe me, it's important. You've got to be comfortable in your own skin to be authentically you, but the clothes you wear, the cars you drive, the colours and the visual element of your brand say a lot to the people you're coming into contact with.

Take relationships, for example. Turning up to a speed dating event in a three-piece suit and patent-leather shoes will give people a certain impression of you, and it'll be different from how you'd come across in shorts, T-shirt and Nikes.

Mark and I have chosen to be very disruptive in our space. When everyone else was wearing badly fitting cheap grey suits and black shoes, we wore tight Italian suits and really bright stripy shirts. I've since traded some of those suits for edgy designer gear (if you've seen me speak, you might have noticed my McQueen swag and Disruptive branded T-shirts) but it's the same on-brand approach, with the aim of getting noticed. We drive red Ferraris and big Lamborghinis, not only because we happen to love them but also because they make a splash.

Putting yourself out there is the key, and how you do that – how you portray the *you* you put out there – will make a real difference in the opportunities you prepare yourself for.

So I challenge you to put yourself out there. Start building and nurturing relationships. Because visibility leads to other things, which lead to other things, which lead to other things …

Some putting-yourself-out-there pointers

I'm going deep on this because it's a big deal for us at the moment – literally. We're on the brink of a big deal because we've put ourselves out there more. It's life changing and all down to visibility.

I think everyone should be focusing on visibility, especially if you want more opportunities in your life. We all struggle with it to some extent – it's not just introverts who shy away from the lime-light. There's always a fear of being judged, making mistakes, not being liked or accepted – even I still get that, and I'm everywhere. This stops us from getting out there more, but it also locks the door to opportunity before it's even had a chance to be opened.

I think you can increase your output. I think you can be more visible. I think you can put yourself out there more. So here are my five top tips:

1 Don't overthink it

Worrying and overthinking is a waste of time – forget your fear of judgement and failure, just do it. Sure, be prepared and do it as well as you can, but get it done.

2 Everything is a test

I take a testing approach to everything – start now, get perfect later. Some things work, some don't. So take step 1 and, if it doesn't work, adjust and try again. Remember, you can always hit delete. This should take the pressure off.

3 What's the worst that could happen?

Seriously, imagine the absolute worst outcome. Now sit with that for a bit. Poke it. Question it. What would you do in that situation? How would you handle it? You'll start to see it from a different perspective and realize nothing is ever that bad. If it happens, you'll learn and move on.

4 Start where you feel comfortable

If you don't know Instagram at all but you're a Facebook pro, forget Instagram for now. If you're a dab hand at video but get dreadful writer's block, choose YouTube over Medium. Start in your niche, your area of expertise, your passion before branching out. Put yourself out there where you feel at home, practice with visibility and then move on to new territory.

5 Get some accountability

What would happen if you didn't put yourself out there? What goals might you not reach by being unprepared for opportunities? Hold on to that, use it to underpin your accountability. Now get some external pressure: a mentor or friend or colleague or coach to make sure you follow through on your plans. Or, even better, public accountability: tell the world what you're going to do and let them hold you to it!

Embrace rejection

Now I'm going to acknowledge the elephant in the room: the negative, judgemental, rejecting troll of an elephant. When you put yourself out there more, you get more visibility and more opportunities. But you also get more criticism, more rejection and even more hate thrown your way.

Don't let this stop you.

Rejection is obviously tough. You could write a whole book on this (*makes a note*). The reality is that people will judge you when you get rejected and watch your reaction closely. If you act like a child in the face of rejection – maybe you get really angry and go into revenge mode – that's going to close opportunities. People won't want to have any kind of exchange with someone who acts like a child when they get rejected. You'll also be shutting out opportunities if you go into hiding when you're rejected or criticized. Remember, visibility is credibility.

This is the thing most people don't understand: it's not about avoiding rejection, it's about learning to deal with it. It's impossible to avoid rejection, especially if you want to be successful in life. I've found that the more successful I've become, the more experience I've got, the more rejection I've had. It just gets bigger and bigger because I've got more to lose, because more people know me, and I've got more people challenging me and demanding things from me.

I've got a thick skin – and I think that it's got thicker the more I've put yourself out there – and I can handle, say, online critics and trolls. I don't take that personally anymore. But if one of my heroes rejected an invitation to be interviewed on my podcast, I would still feel bad about that rejection. It's not like rejection goes away, or even that the fear or the feeling goes away, but you just get to higher levels of dealing with it as you get more successful and more resilient.

I think it's important to acknowledge that even your heroes and idols experienced rejection, and still do. They're just experiencing it at a higher level and they're more resilient to it.

How you do anything is how you do everything. People are judging you all the time. So, in a sense, how you handle rejection will partly define whether you get more or less opportunity in your life.

How should you handle rejection? Always be grateful of feedback, always be grateful of criticism, always accept the 'no', but only accept it today, and then maybe try again tomorrow. When you get knocked down, try again with kindness. Have that persistence, that resilience that people will notice, that quality we all admire because we want it in ourselves. Try to be collaborative as opposed to competitive. Take rejection with a smile on your face. *Own* rejection. Never take it personally.

And remember, you can create opportunity from the rejection. Rejection is, in fact, a really important part of creating the conditions for opportunity. Embrace rejection and you're allowing opportunity to appear. I think if you can handle rejection in this way, the infinite opportunities that you can't see will suddenly open up to you.

Summary

Putting yourself out there is probably the most important thing you can do to create the conditions for opportunity. Whether it's offline at networking events, conferences, meet-ups, parties, the gym, the supermarket or weekly dance classes, or online on Facebook, Instagram, YouTube, forums, Hangouts, Tinder or TikTok, you need to be visible if you want to be credible. I've had massive opportunities – including buying two now very successful companies for very little money – as a direct result of getting out there, being visible and building relationships. Be yourself (although if you're still working on getting to know yourself, that's not an excuse to stay hidden – start now, get perfect later), act with integrity and listen. Every opportunity that appears will come through, with or because of a person you meet.

TAKE ACTION

. . . .

Choose a platform, online or offline, and get out there.

1 *Where do you feel most comfortable?* It could be on Instagram or at your local swimming pool – that doesn't matter.
2 *Make a plan.* Think about what's possible and decide how you're going to use your platform to be more visible, meet people and grow your network. Is it a video on IGTV? Or will you strike up a conversation in the water or under the shower? The plan can be simple: the platform, the content, the date.
3 *Do it.* Don't think too much, don't plan too much, don't live the moment a million times in your head the night before. Hit record, open your mouth, just be you and make a connection.
4 *Celebrate and evaluate.* How do you feel? How did it go? What could you do differently next time? Remember you're taking a testing approach to this, so tweak and try again.
5 Rinse and repeat.

8
Find the balance

Now that I've spent a whole chapter telling you why you should put yourself out there, I'm going to tell you to dial it back in. Everything in life is a paradox, and if you only push, push, push, if you only get in people's faces and chase and shout and work, work, work, you'll push opportunities away. There has to be some balance.

This is about attrition versus attraction – the balance between working hard and letting go, knowing when to hustle and when to leverage, being persistent versus patient. Knowing when to control and when to release.

Think about work. Let's say you want your dream job, coding for Microsoft. You started by applying for the job, then when you were rejected you applied for another one and another one, until you'd applied for every single job advertised, whether it involved coding or not. You called HR every week, then every day. You went to networking events and asked people if they could put a good word in for you. You did extra courses and broadcast your qualifications. You pushed and pushed and pushed until you popped.

Some would say this is the way to go, that you have to keep pushing if you really want something. But I think you need to leave space for opportunities to appear. You need the balance. You need to step back. Without that, you're filling up every inch of your world and leaving no air, no way for anything to breathe or grow. By trying so hard, you're trying too hard – you're pushing people and opportunities away.

Stop ... let go!

Stop pushing, stop chasing. Stop broadcasting and talking and asking for favours. Keep putting yourself out there, but be receptive rather than aggressive – listen. Really listen. Ask questions to learn, not to get something out of people. By doing this, you're opening up some space for opportunity. The things that appear might not be what you'd imagined – perhaps someone offers you an internship at a different company, or a consulting project you hadn't thought of. You need to be ready to spot the opportunities (we'll get to that later), but before they can appear, you need to give them the space to appear.

The same goes for people. Say you want to get a date with a man at the gym, or you want to interview a woman for your podcast. Absolutely go for it – ask him out, invite her for the interview. But if the answer is no, take the no and step back a bit. It's not for ever, and at a certain point it will be time to ask again, but for now you need to stop and let go. If you don't, and you keep asking and asking and chasing and chasing, you'll end up verging on stalker behaviour and you'll look desperate and sad. That's not a good look, and it's not the way to create opportunities. Take the no and use it – make changes, keep putting yourself out there, turn in a different direction.

I see this all the time in parenting. There's a big wave of helicopter parenting, with people wanting to wrap their kids in cotton wool and stop them from ever feeling pain or making mistakes. They hover over their toddlers as they climb in the playground. They read their kids' homework over their shoulders and get stuck in when they get an answer wrong. They drag them to every after-school club going.

Now everyone has their own ways of raising their kids, and I don't claim to be a child development expert (I'm sure my wife would tell you I get it wrong all the time!), but I don't think that's the best approach. Obviously, if you have kids, you love them, you want to look after them and you hate it when they're hurting. But you don't own them. They are not your property. You're responsible for raising them, but you can't live their lives for them. And I'm pretty sure you wouldn't want a 40-something living at home still asking you to do their washing; eventually they'll have to be independent, and you can make it easier on them.

By loosening your grip, even just a bit, you can let them take some control of their own lives. And by letting go, I don't mean abandoning them. Be there to support them through their own decisions. Let your toddler climb, and be there with a hug if they fall. Let your kid get their homework wrong, and be there to support and teach them if they fail.

There's been a lot of research on this. In 2016, a team of psychologists at Florida State University published a study looking at the effect different styles of parenting would have on kids when they grow up into adults. They were interested in helicopter parenting versus what they called autonomy-supportive parenting – essentially when parents support their kids in making their own decisions, like the climbing toddler. They found that kids who were closely controlled by helicopter parents were less competent as adults than those whose parents supported them in making their own decisions. They also found that kids who had supportive parents were more likely to grow up mentally and physically healthy.

I've gone into a bit of detail here, to show you some of the evidence that letting go, loosening your grip, stepping back is beneficial. In the case of parenting, by having such a tight grip, you're squeezing opportunities out for your kid and for you. Imagine all the time and mental space you'd free up if you weren't hovering and trying to live their life, too.

That's what the balance is all about. Knowing when to push, when to squeeze, when to control, when to run, and knowing when to relax, when to let go, when to step back and let space open up.

Don't get me wrong, I'm not saying you should be lazy. I'm not saying that you can lie back and watch Netflix and wait for all the great stuff to happen. That would be swinging too far in the other direction. Do nothing and nothing will happen; you won't learn or meet people or change anything. Opportunity won't have the chance to appear. But if you *never* take that break, if you *always* push, you won't give it room to appear. You need to leave space for things to develop in unforeseen directions.

Forget the hustle

This isn't a trendy thing to say, but it's what I really believe. All this obsession in the business and personal development world with hustle and grind, with twenty-hour working days and no holidays, with work, work, work and no time to rest is, frankly, bollocks. When COVID-19 hit, there was an immediate rush of people boasting about how much work they were getting done – how many bench presses they'd managed, businesses they'd started and screenplays they'd written. The implication was that, even in the face of a global pandemic, to stop grinding was for quitters. As the year progressed, one thing was clear: sacrificing self-care in favour of the hustle only led in one direction.

Living and breathing work, pushing at a hundred miles an hour all day every day, doesn't guarantee you success. It won't give you all the opportunities and make you win at life. In my opinion, the only thing it is certain to give you is a burnout.

So the advice I'm not going to jump on the bandwagon of giving is that the harder you work, the luckier you get; the harder you work, the more opportunities you create. Because a) you probably think that already, and b) I don't believe that it's true.

Let's be clear, I think if you're not working enough, and you're not putting yourself out there enough, and you're not getting noticed enough, and you're not putting enough energy into something, and you haven't been doing it for long enough, you're likely to have limited opportunity. And so, to that end, of course you should be doing more. But a lot of relentless hustle can lead to overwhelm and burnout. It can lead to mistakes, because you're working so hard that your energy and concentration go down. It can make you stressed and impatient, so you end up lashing out at people, at partners, prospects and clients, at followers and fans on social media.

Not only that, I think it's technically rubbish. It's not possible to prescribe a certain number of hours of grind a day or week or month, because we're all different. We all have our own energy flows and circadian rhythms, and pushing against those can have massively negative effects, including making us mentally and physically ill. Research has linked long working hours to a whole range of health problems, from heart disease to reproductive issues. The constant grind isn't going to help you have a long and healthy life.

Plus, there's clearly no one-size-fits-all answer to the ideal number of working hours. The effects of long working hours on things like sleep and physical and mental health aren't the same for everyone. You have your own capacity for hard work. The global COVID-19 pandemic of 2020 really highlighted this. Not only did it show that a sudden change in working habits impacted people very differently, but also that for a vast number of people, being forced to re-evaluate the hours which they work provided an opportunity in itself – to slow down or speed up, to press pause and reconsider what work means to them, and how much of it they should do.

I don't know how many hours a day you could realistically work – it might be 18 (I doubt it) or it might be four – but once you hit that limit, your effectiveness takes a nosedive. The quality of your work falls. You make mistakes, you damage relationships, you close the door to opportunity.

And you're probably kidding yourself, too. Even if people think they're working 12 hours a day, they're likely only working four or five hours and procrastinating the rest of the time. This has been shown time and time again – people report working 60, 70, 80 hours a week when, in reality, they're not even working the equivalent of a normal full-time job.

This procrastination 'padding' – this filling up your time with junk – only serves to fill up your time. It's not productive or effective.

I think what's even more important than working hard (or long) is working smart.

Work smart

Back in 2007, a book hit the shelves with a premise that shocked the world. It's pretty mainstream now, but back then it was really ground-breaking. The idea was that you could succeed in business by working four hours a week. *WHAT?! Four hours a week? And spend the rest of the time sipping cocktails on a white sandy beach? Sign me up!*

The book was by Tim Ferriss, an American entrepreneur and activist. He was hustling at the time, burning himself out, and decided there had to be a better way. He started outsourcing tasks to a team of virtual assistants and setting aside specific timeframes for working on emails and so on. It worked for him, so he wrote down his approach and shared it in a book – *The 4-Hour Workweek*. It inspired the world: it has sold two million copies in 40 languages and spent more than four years on the *New York Times* Best Seller list.

Is everyone doing it? No. Why? It's weirdly easier to work hard and hustle and push than it is to take a step back, delegate and create space.

But knowing when to work hard and when to work smart – and actually doing it – is really critical if you want to invite opportunity into your life.

I think Tim Ferriss was maybe a bit extreme (I'd bet you'd actually be missing out on opportunities by only working four hours a week), but he had a point. And it's something that underpins the content in my book *Life Leverage*. Forget the hustle and the grind – it's about working and living smart, making space for opportunities.

Life Leverage is full of practical tips and exercises to help you work (and live) smart and get the most out of your time. I'll share some of the approaches in Part 3, but I'll explain the idea a bit more now.

For a start, I don't buy the traditional advice that you need to master a skill before outsourcing it or hiring someone to do it. You can't do everything; you have to let go to grow. If you want to grow a company, for example, you won't succeed by constantly working harder and doing everything yourself. You need to hire great people, forge partnerships and collaborations and joint ventures. You need to let go of the control and ownership and the tasks and the roles and the projects, and hand some of that over to the people you hire, who are capable of doing a good job. To master the growth of a company, to take it to the next level, you have to get out of their way and give them autonomy and let them make strategic decisions.

This means letting go of that belief that only you can do the job well, that the clients only want you, that your way is the only way. What you realize as you grow a business is that when you hire brilliant people, who are smarter than you and better than you at the job, they have better results and a wider reach and more sales and higher-quality outputs. Once you let go of control and your ego (well, not all of it), you will really start to see results.

Do this again and again and you'll be multiplying the good work you can get done. Let's say your capacity is five hours a day; if you work hard and well for those five hours, that will give you 35 hours a week of good work. But if you have ten employees doing the same, that's 350 hours of work being done. That has all come from you working *smarter*, not *harder*.

The same applies to other areas of your life, too. If it takes you a whole day to do the housework, are you really doing your best or is a lot of that time wasted by pottering around getting distracted? Would it be more efficient and, in the end, a better investment to pay a cleaner for a few hours a week? If you're in the gym for three hours at a time, are you really using that time or are you floating around unsure of what you should be doing? Would it be better to hire a trainer for an hour a week to keep you efficient and on track?

Fitness is a really good example. Any trainer will tell you that if you train flat out, at 100 per cent, every day, you'll end up doing more harm than good. You'll over-train, tear muscle, injure yourself. The same goes for diet – if you starve yourself, you'll put your body into survival mode and end up storing more fat. If you do everything at once – if you cut calories, run ten miles a day, lift weights – you won't see the results you need. Everything is about balance. A rest day is just as important as a training day; you need to eat to survive.

It's all about balance.

Of course, you still need to work hard. Without hard work, you won't get anywhere in business. You won't get fitter or healthier or learn another language or meet the love of your life. But working so hard you leave no space for opportunities to develop will work against you.

People do this on a micro-level, too, with things like the Pomodoro Technique.* I use this for my writing … in fact, I've got a break coming up now. Back in five minutes.

Here I am again, refreshed and ready to roll. When I'm writing, I write solidly for 25 minutes and then take a five-minute break. Working 25 minutes doesn't seem hard or unachievable; it's much less stressful than telling myself I need to work for a month and write 60,000 words. By chopping up my writing time into bitesize chunks, I keep myself rolling, I stay sharp and the writing doesn't tail off. You can read exhaustion, I think.

So instead of hustling, be more creative. Instead of being prolific, be patient, take time and space and allow ideas to come to you instead of filling every minute of your day with tasks and padding.

Make space … literally

Your opportunities aren't just being hampered by padding out your time and energy – it's your physical space, too. Any minimalist will

---

*Time-management technique developed by the Italian Francesco Cirillo in the late 1980s, named after the tomato-shaped timer Cirillo used as a motivational technique when working as a student.

tell you that their lives became infinitely better when they ditched their addiction to material objects and cleared out their lives. You don't need to sell everything and move into a tiny house, or cut your wardrobe down to 30 items, or do a total clear-out, Marie Kondo style (though, yes, that speaker does spark joy) to feel the benefits of decluttering.

This is something I do every few months: I take one full day off and clear out my life. Really. It's my colonic irrigation for the soul (you're welcome, that's a great picture you've got of me in your head now).

By clearing out my physical environment, I clear out my energy. I reset whatever bad fumes are lingering from burning the midnight oil (because no matter how smart I work, just like everyone, I also fall into the trap of doing too much). It's like productive meditation.

I'll take you through my process:

1 About a month before I start, I get a whole team involved. I ask my wife to get involved, I tell the kids to start separating out toys they don't play with, I tell the gardener to spruce things up outside, I tell the cleaner to start bagging things (one bag for 'important', one for 'not sure', one for 'probably junk').

2 On Irrigation Day, I first hit my wardrobe. You wear 20 per cent of your clothes 80 per cent of the time. I look through and anything that isn't getting used I sell or take to the charity shop.

3 Then I go wider and look at my physical surroundings. I get rid of the lot! (Not really, I'm a collector at heart, so God help anyone if they touch my vinyl records ...) It's important for me to have a space I enjoy, and that feels zen and conducive to me being productive. I take away anything that's not important and not being used, that's broken or no longer needed. Toys, old magazines, books. I always

find coins (where do they come from?!) – I stick change into a big bottle for the kids.†

4 I look at where I'm storing (hoarding) things – loft, basement, behind the sofa – and give everything I don't need to charity.

5 I clean my car. I make sure there's change in the car for parking and that it's a nice, clear place to be.

6 Then it's the digital stuff. I clear my email (do you dare to go Brian Tracy style: select 'all', hit 'delete'?) and make sure my filing system makes sense. I unsubscribe to email lists. I clear out all my direct debits and subscriptions. I fix everything and sync everything. I make sure all my systems are working – music, software, remote control everything.

7 I back everything up. I make sure I have a spare set of keys. I back up my phone, computer and other devices. I get spare memory cards and batteries. I put together a travel bag for my laptop with a charger and headphones, and I have a second set ready. That way, if anything goes wrong, or if an opportunity comes up, I'm prepared.

8 The last thing I do, when everything is decluttered and calm, is connect. I message all my friends, the people I care about, and tell them I care about them. Take time out to give some love to the people who matter, because they'll always be there.

Fun, right? If you're well prepared, you can whizz through the steps in a day. Don't hang around, don't think too much, don't agonize over things, this isn't an episode of *Hoarders*.

When you declutter your life, you declutter your mind. You can think straight. You're clear. That means people will buy into your vision because they will understand it – you can communicate

---

†Here's a good opportunity to get smart about money: save the big change yourself and hide all your £5 notes (or dollars or euros or whatever your equivalent is). Saving small money teaches you to manage your bigger money. Then you can go and buy physical assets with it and so on.

clearly and inspire other people. If you're decluttered and open, you will attract more into your life and people, things and opportunities will radiate towards you.

Summary

You need to strike a balance and know when to push and when to step back. Pushing and controlling will leave no space for opportunities to appear. This goes for every area of your life – push a love interest too hard and they'll run away. Push too hard with your diet or training and you'll get injured. Work too hard or too long and you'll end up filling your time with procrastination padding, making mistakes and probably harming your health. Instead, be smart. Leverage your time, delegate tasks, declutter and create some space – physical, mental and spiritual – in your life. Only then will you create an environment where opportunity can arrive.

TAKE ACTION

. . . .

1 *Write a leverage list.* Where in your life can you find opportunities for working smart, not hard? Can you outsource or delegate tasks? Is there anywhere you can get rid of the padding?

2 *Declutter.* You could go the whole hog and try my colonic irrigation of the soul, or you could choose one area to start with. Declutter your life and see how it feels. I can guarantee you'll want to do more.

9

Fill up your brain …

Think about an opportunity you took recently. What knowledge let that opportunity happen or let you take it? What did you know, what had you learned, to make it an opportunity for you?

Did you have the technical knowledge to take the job? Or the business acumen to make the deal? Or the acting skills to get the part? Or the emotional intelligence to help a friend?

I believe knowledge is one of the most important things in life. Full stop. Whatever your profession, passion, position or personality, I guarantee you can improve your life beyond measure by learning.

Education versus learning

Now, I want to make a distinction right from the start between education and learning. This is a pretty hot topic in my communities online, particularly the Disruptive Entrepreneurs Community on Facebook. This distinction really comes down to the source of the information: by education I mean getting a qualification from an institution like a university; by learning I mean gaining knowledge from anywhere.

People often ask me if I would recommend they, or their child, should go to university. I always ask them what direction they want their lives to go in. If they want to become a doctor, surgeon or dentist, a lawyer, accountant or any other certified profession, I say go to university. It's the right, proven path.

But if they want to be an entrepreneur, I say steer clear of university.

Here's my reasoning: university could hold you back five years. While everyone else is studying, you could be gaining really valuable experience (that's the learning I'm talking about), earning money and getting prepared for the opportunities that could help you start and grow your business. By the time the graduates are ready to start applying for jobs, you'll be years ahead of them, working where degrees no longer matter. And you won't be up to your eyeballs in debt.

I went to university to study architecture. When I applied, I was convinced that's what I wanted to do, but looking back I was clueless and trying to fill a hole I hadn't even looked into yet. My parents were really happy and my friends were all doing the same thing, so it seemed like what I should be doing.

I don't regret things in life, but one of the very few things I would do differently given another chance is this: I wouldn't go to university. My degree was a waste of time – it set me back seven years, because what I studied ended up being totally irrelevant when I figured out what I actually wanted to do.

I think there are tons of benefits to going the life learning route rather than the education route. You can stay living at home until you've saved enough or are earning enough to support yourself (as long as your parents let you, that is), which means you don't have to live in halls of residence or a frat house or a shared student rental, where you get to listen to pumping music (or hips …) night and day, enjoy the aromas of cheap deodorant and even cheaper microwave meals, and try to figure out who stole your [enter item of food or clothing here].

Can you tell that I loved my university experience?

If you don't go to university, you can direct your own learning. Instead of going to lectures and other classes, you can put your time into seeking out entrepreneurs and learning from them. Soak up their knowledge, their wisdom. Get them to mentor you if you can, or at least answer a few questions. You can look for role models who are living at the level you want to reach, then consume their content – listen to, watch and read them. Squeeze every last drop of knowledge out of them.

There are plenty of hugely successful entrepreneurs who didn't go to university, or who dropped out before they graduated, so I'm in good company. Bill Gates and Steve Jobs both quit before completing in order to set up Microsoft and Apple. With a net worth of $110 billion, Bill Gates is the world's most successful dropout. Fast-forward a few decades and Mark Zuckerberg did the same thing, to set up Facebook, which is now worth over $500 billion.

This probably isn't new information to you – these three names tend to be at the top of the list whenever the value of a degree is being debated. But they're not alone. In 2015, data analysis company Wealth-X did a billionaire census, which revealed almost 30 per cent of the world's billionaires didn't have a bachelor's degree. That's a surprising 739 out of 2,473 billionaires.

Of course, that also means that the remaining 70 per cent did have a degree. And, although I personally believe you don't need a degree to succeed in business, I'm sure many of these people would have positive experiences to share.

One defence that's used a lot when this debate appears online is that most professional jobs require a university degree these days. Why? The theory goes that, even if the subject isn't relevant (which is often the case), it's the achievement – the persistence and effort and ability to learn that are displayed in the qualification – that says a lot about a person right off the bat.

Even if you're qualified, a degree won't guarantee you a job. An estimated 5 per cent of graduates are unemployed. However, unemployment increases as level of education decreases, so the higher level of education you achieve, the more likely you are to have a job. You can see a reversal of this pattern in earnings, too – the higher your education, the more you're likely to earn.

I get the appeal of a degree as a filter for job applications, but I don't agree with using it that way. I've hired hundreds of people, and I think there are hundreds of better ways to judge someone. We're moving further away from traditional working structures and the nine to five and towards relatively new setups like the gig economy. This means people are evaluating their own experiences differently. In a 2018 survey, freelancers in the USA valued the skills they learned on the job more highly than their degrees.

In my experience as an entrepreneur and through my conversations with other entrepreneurs, I'm confident in saying a degree won't get you all that far if you're setting up a business. You'd be much better off putting together your own programme of learning, starting with people whose footsteps look like the path you want to tread.

A good way to start doing that is to read, read and read some more.

Reading expands the mind

The world's most successful dropout is also one of its most prolific readers. Bill Gates carries around a bag of hard-copy books with him, which he dips into whenever he has a spare minute. He reads fast (about 150 pages an hour, according to a documentary about him★) and retains an astounding amount of information. He reads books about anything and everything, from economic theory to epidemiology. He's interested and has a thirst for knowledge.

Gates is one of the many successful people, billionaires, entrepreneurs and CEOs who read as if their lives depended on it. You've probably come across articles listing the books that Warren Buffett, Oprah Winfrey, Richard Branson and many others have read, shouting about the benefits of reading every day, and claiming that these celebs read hundreds of pages a day – *and so should you!*

There's a lot of sense in this. There's a famous saying, 'A person who won't read has no advantage over one who can't read.' It's true – if you're not applying it, what's the use in having that skill? It's not everyone's cup of tea at first, but reading can be life changing. As Oprah said: 'What I know for sure is that reading opens you up. It exposes you and gives you access to anything your mind

---

★ *Inside Bill's Brain: Decoding Bill Gates* (Netflix, 2019), directed by Davis Guggenheim.

can hold. What I love most about reading [is that it] gives you the ability to reach higher ground.'

That was definitely the case for me. Now, I'm not going to be hardcore about this. I don't read 500 pages a day like Warren Buffett. I don't carry around a bag of books like Bill Gates. But I do read a lot. I don't tend to read hard copies these days, but I listen to loads of audiobooks (on 2x speed) and to the summaries of books on Blinkist.

I really started reading more when I first jumped into property – I was devouring books on money and biographies of successful people. The more I read, the more I realized I could learn a lot from these people, so the more I read. As I continued to change and grow, my reading expanded. I read about different areas of life and business, I read about people I didn't know, in industries I had no connection to.

One great reader, former US Secretary of Defense General James Mattis, has a library of 7,000 books at home. He is quoted as having said: 'You stay teachable most by reading books, by reading what other people went through.' And that's exactly the point. It's not just about learning but keeping the door open to more learning. By staying teachable, your mind is open, your brain is working, and you're prepared for opportunity.

You're obviously on board with this, because you're reading this book, but if you need more convincing, I've put together a list of my favourite books on a range of topics:

Rob's reading list

Total Recall: My Unbelievably True Life Story by Arnold Schwarzenegger and Peter Petre
Finding the Next Steve Jobs: How to Find, Keep and Nurture Creative Talent by Gene Stone and Nolan Bushnell
Influence: The Psychology of Persuasion by Robert Cialdini
Uncommon Sense: The popular misconceptions of business, investing and finance and how to profit by going against the tide by Mark Homer
The Power of Now by Eckhart Tolle

Hustle Harder, Hustle Smarter by Curtis Jackson
Money by Rob Moore
The Art of Happiness by Dalai Lama XIV and Howard C. Cutler
The Upstarts: How Uber, Airbnb, and the Killer Companies of the New Silicon Valley Are Changing the World by Brad Stone
Total Rethink: Why Entrepreneurs Should Act Like Revolutionaries by David McCourt
Breaking The Habit of Being Yourself: How to Lose Your Mind and Create a New One by Joe Dispenza
The Rise and Fall… and Rise Again by Gerald Ratner
The Gratitude Effect by John Demartini
Traction by Gino Wickman

Learn how to learn

I soak up a huge amount of knowledge from books, but that's not the only way I learn. I listen to podcasts, I watch documentaries, I read magazines and watch YouTube videos. Most importantly, I talk to people. I ask questions. I listen.

I haven't always been such an active learner. When I was at school, I didn't exactly struggle, but I excelled far more in creative subjects like art (I was apparently the only person in my year to get 100 per cent in my art GCSE). That hands-on, artsy way of doing things appealed to me. I liked getting physically stuck in, instead of sticking my head in a book. I preferred paintbrushes to calculators.

Now, looking back, it's so obvious that my creative streak was totally in line with becoming an entrepreneur. I think something people don't realize is that succeeding in business requires huge amounts of creativity: you need a flow of ideas across every aspect of the business, from the product to the marketing; you need creative solutions to difficult problems, creative ways to change with the times, creative ways to find the right people.

Creativity isn't one-way – you don't just create, it's not all output. You also need input. You need to learn. The more you learn, the better you get. In art, the more you know about art history, about colour theory, about techniques and tools, about light and texture, the better your art will be – not because you'll apply everything you know, but because you'll have a deeper appreciation of the things you do apply. The same thing applies to writing: when a novelist learns a lot about a certain topic, that knowledge seeps through to improve their writing, even if they don't include the detail in the book.

In business, the more you know about every aspect of your niche, your industry, your brand, the more you understand finance and marketing and operations, the more you know about hiring (and firing) people, about different ways businesses have done things throughout time and across industries, about their failures and successes, the more successful you'll be.

I believe I can learn business from every niche. I love learning from fashion, I love learning from music, I love learning from art, and I love putting aspects of all that into my business models, which are not in those niches. I love learning from competitors, and I love learning from people. I love hanging around with young people because it makes me feel young. I love hanging around with older people, who are old enough to be my dad or my granddad, because they've got more life experience than me. I love learning from people in different cultures because they have different outlooks.

Here are eight ways to learn something *right now*:

1 Consciously try to learn something from the next three people you speak to. Instead of making small talk, ask them real, meaningful or even surprising questions. Listen actively and make a note of whatever you learned.
2 Look around you and spot something you could read that would teach you something new. It could be a newspaper or magazine, a book or a website. Choose something

out of your area of expertise and read until you've come across something new.

3　Watch a TED Talk. Go to ted.com and look for something that interests you – or, if you're up for it, ask the site to surprise you. I guarantee you'll learn something in less than 18 minutes.

4　Sign up for an online course. There are thousands of free courses online (like Coursera or Stanford Online), and even more for a small payment (think Udemy or LinkedIn Learning). Choose something related to your work, a hobby or another interest. Do the first session.

5　Think about something that went wrong in your life or work in the last week. Write down three things you can take away from that.

6　Listen to a podcast. There are millions of podcast episodes out there – you can learn anything from ancient history to parenting to marketing to short-story writing and way beyond. Choose a podcast you haven't listened to before and listen to an episode. Make a note of what you learned.

7　Contact someone you want to learn from – someone you respect or look up to. It could be a mentor figure or even a friend or family member. You might know them, or they could be a stranger. Ask them a question and listen to their answer.

8　Quiz a community. Think of something you want to learn and ask the hive mind: post in a Facebook group (like the Disruptive Entrepreneurs Community), or a LinkedIn group, or an online forum, and learn from people's comments.

The more you listen and the more you see everyone and everything as an opportunity to learn from, then all of a sudden, opportunities flow through them and to you. Use the thing you've learned here about connecting with people and be a sponge.

Summary

The more you learn, the more prepared you'll be for opportunity. Use every opportunity to learn – talk to people, listen and, above all, read! Reading will broaden your horizons and give you in-depth knowledge in all sorts of areas. Choose hard copies, eBooks or audiobooks – and start with my reading list if you need a boost.

TAKE ACTION

. . . .

Discover your reading style and learn from three books.

If you already know how you prefer to read, great! You can skip step 2. If you're not sure, go through all the steps.

1 Choose three books to read, which you've never read before. Choose one in your niche (whatever area of life that's in – business, parenting, fitness, hobbies ...), one in a totally different niche and one fiction book.

2 Choose a different format for each book. One could be hard copy, one eBook, one audiobook, for example.

3 Read them all – one by one, in parallel, one in each hand and one on your lap, however you do it, do it fast. Aim to read them all within three weeks. (Want to level up? Try one week.) As you read, take notes of anything you're learning. It might be straight-up information, lessons, ideas or inspiration.

4 Distil what you learned from each book onto a single notecard, so you have three cards at the end.

5 Look at the results to see what type of reading worked best for you. What did you enjoy most, and what did you learn most from? Try reading this way again and see if you have the same experience.

10

... And now empty your brain

Have you figured out yet that I believe everything is a paradox? If you're filling up on information, learning, soaking up knowledge from people and events and books and documentaries, then you have to take time to empty everything out again and give your brain a bit of a breather.

Don't worry, I'm not going to get all woo-woo here. I don't claim for a minute to be some kind of zen monk – I don't sit cross-legged on top of a mountain in my pants once a week and breathe in and out until I'm enlightened. I'm also not saying that that's not a great thing to do; I'm just not monk material. I'd be like a monk on speed, I reckon. After 41 years of getting to know myself, I've accepted that I have two speeds: fast and warp speed. Not very monkish.

But that doesn't mean I don't think it's absolutely vital to meditate and be mindful and give your brain space for imagination.

Walking as meditation

Meditation looks different for everyone. For the monk who is capable of slowing down, it's sitting cross-legged on a mountain. For the woman who needs a time out from her high-pressure c-suite job, it's running before sunrise. For the man who's trying to get a start-up off the ground, it's digging up the garden. For the teenager under pressure to be the next master concert pianist, it's walking along a beach, watching the rhythmic crash of the waves.

For me, it's walking.

I tried meditation. I tried mindfulness. I can't do it! I'm too impatient, I just end up thinking, 'When is this going to end?!'

I was determined to make it happen because I know the value of switching off. I followed guided meditations, I read books, I watched videos, I tried loads of tips from people. I really wanted to make it work. I wanted to sit there and get that zen feeling people talk about. I wanted to empty my mind, focus on my brain and let the magic happen. AAAAARGH, it was so frustrating!

If you've seen me, you might have noticed that I'm kind of wired. I'm constantly moving. I'm really physical when I talk, I move my arms and my hands, and I like to walk around when I talk. If I'm sitting down, I'm upright, alert, and one of my legs is probably bouncing up and down at a million miles an hour. I'm not a still person. Trying to force myself into being still was like trying to fit a constantly morphing peg into a square hole.

But I didn't give up. Why? A full brain can't get ideas. A full brain can't think outside the box. A full brain can't see opportunities. I need to be able to do all of those things – I think we all do. And the more I stuffed my brain full of knowledge and insights and other people's experiences, the more I developed my own skills, and the more I did, day after day, the more that was building up and leaving less and less space.

The thing that has ended up being a huge positive influence in my life and work started sort of accidentally. I was feeling a bit overloaded and stressed, so I went for a walk. I felt better. I went for a walk the next day. Same thing.

That's the way habits are built – repeated actions with positive results. Over the days, weeks and months, this has become a regular part of my routine. I walk for about an hour and a half a day. It gives me loads of benefits:

- It's healthy and I get some exercise.
- It makes me breathe more deeply – and fresh air, not recycled office air.

- It gives me time to make calls – I usually do 15-minute one-to-one coaching or mentoring calls, often free for people in my communities online.
- It's an opportunity to clear my head, to just walk, take in the scenery and let my mind wander.

This last point is the big one. Walking has become my meditation. I do use some of the time for connecting, but I always use some of it for emptying my brain. I find that 'meditating' while walking doesn't make me impatient; I don't get jumpy and I can really see the thoughts and ideas getting some space and starting to flow.

After my walk, I'm focused, full of energy and more open. I notice more. I listen better. I've cleared out all the crap that was flying around in my head, and quite often I've solved problems that were taking up space without having to think about them too hard (or, even better, someone else has solved them while I've been walking – but don't tell my team about that little trick).

This head space is so valuable. It's like hitting reset, like shaking the Etch A Sketch (now I'm showing my age). It can literally bring you money, by inviting opportunity in the form of ideas.

Ideas are opportunities. Every time you have an idea, it's an opportunity to make something, change something, solve something, do something, transform something. Like an opportunity, an idea can be good or bad or somewhere in between; it can appear at the right time or the wrong time.

Ideas can't be forced. You can't sit down and decide you're going to have an idea. You can have thoughts, make connections, take a new perspective on something, but real ideas come to you when your mind is open to them.

That's why so many people have ideas in the shower (presumably someone got the idea for the waterproof shower whiteboard while in the shower!). And, as the story goes, the word we say when we get a great idea – 'eureka', was first said by the ancient Greek mathematician Archimedes when he was in the bath. Taking time out to wash seems to be a great way to have ideas. So stay clean, folks!

Seriously though, it's when we're doing these mundane, routine, repetitive things – sitting and breathing, taking one step after another, washing our hair – that we stop actively thinking and start leaving space in our brains.

The boredom paradox

There's another really important element to letting ideas – and therefore opportunities – happen: boredom. One group of psychologists defined boredom as 'the aversive experience of wanting, but being unable, to engage in satisfying activity'.* That's an expensive way of saying doing nothing, and getting no satisfaction from it. We fight boredom. Next time you're somewhere you have to wait – in a queue in the post office or supermarket, on a bus or a train, at the airport or doctor's waiting room – look around you. How many people are literally doing nothing? I'll bet none of them. I'll bet most people will be on their phones, and a few might be leafing through a magazine or talking to someone.

Modern society has made it really easy for us to fight boredom. First, everyone and everything around us is saying we should squeeze all we can out of every moment of our lives. We're being sold efficiency devices and apps, programs that will help us learn German while we're boiling the kettle or watch the latest TV series while we're on the toilet (*The Good Place* is brilliant, by the way). Stuck waiting for a delayed train? No problem, just head

---

*J. D. Eastwood, A. Frischen, M. J. Fenske and D Smilek, 'The unengaged mind', *Perspectives on Psychological Science* 7.5 (2012): 482–95.

down a YouTube hole that starts with the latest State of the Union speech by the US president and ends with a microwave popcorn taste test. That'll fill the time – and hey, you'll learn something about popcorn. Got nothing to do before your hair appointment? That's OK, Candy Crush has your back.

It's so automatic now to pull out our phones or reach for the nearest distraction at the first, smallest hint of boredom. Even if we're working on something and start to get a bit bored, we open yet another browser tab, or check Facebook, or send a message.

Of course we do that! Boredom is painful. Unpleasant. Why wouldn't we try to avoid painful, unpleasant feelings?

Well, for one thing, because being bored is brilliant for inviting opportunities.

Canadian psychologist Professor John Eastwood, whose defi-nition of boredom I shared just now, has been studying boredom for two decades, and he's a big fan. In fact, he thinks we should be bored more often. Eastwood says that boredom happens when we can't focus our attention on information, and we feel the need to do something satisfying, whether that's internal (like thoughts and feelings) or external (like smartphones and books and tele-vision). We then blame our environment for this terrible state of boredom.

People often don't like to admit they get bored. It's like a badge of honour to never be bored. You've probably come across them, those people who are so interested in everything and everyone and fill every nook of their lives with something wonderful and meaningful. But it's a load of crap. Everybody gets bored. I get bored. I get bored all the time. You get bored all the time. The trick is sometimes we need to embrace it rather than fix it.

Like everything in life, this is a big paradox. On the one hand I'm saying you can leverage the shit out of your life to make every moment count, to learn as much as you can, and on the other hand I'm saying stop, leave space, *get bored*.

There's a reason for this.

According to psychologists, being bored serves a really important purpose. Dr Wijnand van Tilburg, from the University of Southampton, said in an interview for *The Psychologist* that '... boredom makes people keen to engage in activities that they find more meaningful than those at hand. Essentially, the unpleasant sensation of boredom "reminds" people that there are more important matters to attend to than those at hand.'

Being bored helps you realize what really matters. It helps you gain some perspective; it gives you an insight into what's meaningful. As Professor Eastwood put it, we should be treating boredom as an opportunity to 'discover the possibility and content of one's desires.'

What could be more boring than sitting in a confined space for months? Astronauts know this situation well. After spending four months in a NASA Mars mission simulation, journalist Kate Greene wrote in an essay for the digital ideas magazine *Aeon*: 'On Mars I learned that boredom has two sides – it can either rot the mind or rocket it to new places.'

Obviously, I don't want your mind to rot; what we're after here is the rocketing. And I think boredom has huge potential. You need to get bored in order to attract opportunities.

Think about it. If you're all go-go-go all the time, life won't get in edgeways. Opportunities will just bounce off you. You'll be the proverbial speeding bullet and you won't stop until you hit an opportunity head on. And then you'll probably kill it.

Instead, get bored. Stop chasing satisfying activities. Get some perspective and let yourself see what's meaningful.

I hate being bored just as much as the next person; probably more, actually. And I get bored easily. Life needs to be moving *fast* to keep hold of my attention. I want things to happen yesterday. I want results *now*. But I'm aware of how important boredom is, so I have a few ways I make it happen. Maybe they'll help you too.

Leave space in your diary

I block time for certain important activities on a daily, weekly, monthly and yearly basis. And that includes blocking nothing. Time with nothing to fill it. Time to invite boredom, let serendipity happen, embrace nothingness.

Notice when you switch tasks

This is easier on some days than others – I spend a lot of my time in meetings and interviews, travelling around and broadcasting, and I'm constantly switching what I'm doing. But think about when you're trying to focus on something and end up somewhere else; try to notice it and think about whether you can let yourself be bored for a while. If you're waiting somewhere and your automatic response to the mind space is to fill it, question what you're about to do and maybe just get bored.

Whether it's through meditation or inviting boredom, I hope I've convinced you that having an empty brain is just as important as filling it up by learning. I think you'll see some really amazing things start to happen when you make the space.

Summary

Now that you've filled up your brain, you need to empty it. There's a reason so many people talk about meditation and mindfulness as being life changing – slowing down your brain will give opportunities a fighting chance of showing up. Meditation can look different to different people – it might be sitting cross-legged on a yoga mat, but it might be washing up or walking. Find your meditation. You need to do this to let ideas happen, and ideas are opportunities. Invite boredom – get uncomfortable, fight distraction, let opportunity in.

TAKE ACTION
. . . .
Find your meditation.

How do you empty your brain? Go to YouTube or Spotify or your podcast app and find a guided meditation. If you've never tried it before, start small – ten minutes is fine.

Note how you feel at the start. Are you stressed? Is your mind buzzing? Write it down. Then find yourself a quiet place, where you can be alone and be comfortable, and follow the meditation. At the end, make another note of how you're feeling. Did it have an effect? How did you experience it?

Try this every day for a week, then decide if you want to continue. If you do, great! If not, try the next thing, and try it every day for a week. Here are some ideas: go for a run, knit, swim, dig a hole, wash the dishes, walk. Make it something that's repetitive and that doesn't require active concentration. What's your meditation?

11

Step outside your comfort zone

Now that you're all zen, I want you to wake yourself up with something new.

Have you ever noticed that the people who seem to get a lot of opportunities are the ones who take risks? Who are never sitting still in their lives? Who are always trying new things? It makes sense when you think about it – if you do the same things with the same people in the same places day in day out, you're massively limiting your opportunities. And if you did the opposite … if you tried new things all the time, met new people, went to new places, what would happen then?

You might be rejected by the new people. You might fail at the new thing. You might not like the new place. It might feel bad, painful, embarrassing.

But it might be amazing. You might meet new friends, business partners, love interests. You might find your calling. You might completely fall for the new place and make it home.

Fear of the unknown is a strong thing. Our brains go to the worst possible outcomes straight away. And that's good, that's healthy. There's a reason for that – it's biological. Fear is the most primal emotion, and it's there to protect us from lions and volcanic eruptions and people who might want to kill us. But let's face it, Derek from the networking event doesn't want to kill you. So why let that fear stop you from doing new things?

I have a sort of catchphrase that I say all the time: if you don't risk anything, you risk everything. I've built my life on this. It's such a central idea to me – if you take no risks, if you never try anyway despite the fear, if you never get uncomfortable, you won't be ready for opportunities.

OK, I want you to imagine yourself in your comfort zone right now. Look around you:

- Where are you? At home? At the office? In the same country/city/village you've always lived?
- Who are you with? Your family? Friends? Colleagues?
- What are you doing? Cooking? Working? Playing with the kids? At the gym?

Now I want you to go back to what you wrote down at the end of Chapter 2 – are those all the opportunities that you have right now, here in your comfort zone?

Now I want you to imagine your comfort zone dissolve away into a blank screen. You can put back a few absolutely essential elements (your family, for example) but you're going to change everything else:

- Choose a new, unknown location. A different house? A different workplace? A new country?
- Who are you with now? I want you to imagine people you don't (yet) know.
- What are you doing? Make this something new – a totally new career direction or a massive leap forward, a new hobby or something you've always wanted to try.

Now look at the list of opportunities. What's changed? What might have opened up for you? A new job, business opportunity or collaboration? A new connection, partner, baby? A trip or activity that's not in your reach right now?

What I'm trying to get you to explore in your imagination is the opportunities that can open up if you get out of your comfort zone. The opportunities that surround you right now are probably not ones you want to take, otherwise you will have taken them already. New ones won't just appear from nowhere unless you make a change in your life.

This exercise might have made you nervous – sometimes just imaging change can raise your heart rate. If that's the case, embrace it. Enjoy the flow of blood. Feel the tingle. As we saw in Part 1, you can turn that fear into excitement. Try to feel how exciting it could be to take a risk, to step out of your comfort zone and let new things unfold.

Go where no one else dares

Most people live in their comfort zones quite happily their whole lives. I'm sure you know that old couple who have been in their house for more than 60 years, have always been married to each other, and eat dinner at the same time every day in front of the same TV programmes. They are content – that's what they want. And if that makes them happy, that's great!

But is that what you want? Because if you snuggle into your comfort zone too well, that's what will end up happening.

Not everyone ends up living a long and happy life with their partner in their family home by staying in their comfort zone; actually your comfort zone might be full of pain and negativity and trauma. Either way, people don't usually want to upset the balance and make change. Change is scary. Change is risky. It's a case of the better the devil you know.

Change brings opportunity.

The way to max out on your opportunities, to really create the conditions for opportunity to appear, is to embrace change, seek out challenges, do the things others don't dare to do.

If you're doing the actions at the end of each chapter, you've already taken a step in this direction by putting yourself out there more. (If you're not, flip back to the start and stop cheating! I'm watching you …) How did it feel? I'm willing to bet that you'll notice new opportunities almost instantly. Imagine how powerful change can be when you apply it to other areas of your life.

I'm always pushing myself out of my comfort zone, in every area of my life. Take fitness, for example. When I turned 40, I looked at myself in the mirror, then took off my rose-tinted comfort-zone glasses, then looked again, then cried, then set up a fitness challenge.

I went into my groups on social media and asked who would be interested in taking part in a challenge. Big risk, bigger reward. We would all put in £500 and then spend 12 weeks really pushing ourselves to get in shape, holding each other accountable through a WhatsApp group. The person who lost the most body weight in those 12 weeks would take the pot of money – thousands of pounds.

I was leaving my comfort zone in so many ways. I was being vulnerable about being unhappy with my body, I was putting myself out there, I was committing to a really difficult challenge, and I was asking strangers to hold me accountable. Instead of sticking with my squidgy belly (which was really comfortable!) I jumped at a challenge.

The risk paid off. Not financially, I lost my £500 to a very worthy winner. But I came away from that challenge feeling fit, proud and confident.

That's a really important point. People talk about needing confidence to get out of their comfort zones, make changes and try something new, but I think it's the opposite process: by getting out of your comfort zone, making changes and doing something new, you're building your confidence.

Start a confidence spiral

The more confident you get, the more you'll challenge yourself and the more confident you'll get, and so on. It's a self-driving spiral that will boost your opportunities like you wouldn't believe.

Trying new things that challenge you or make you grow is one of five things I think you can do to be more confident:

1 Talk yourself up, not down.
2 Try things that make you grow or challenge you.

3 Try to master something.

4 Honour all the things you've done or are great at already.

5 Review what you do well and what you fail at doing.

Let's look at these in more detail:

1 Talk yourself up, not down

This applies internally and externally. We all have negative self-talk in some areas of our lives (if you don't, you're either mega-confident or a psychopath ... which is it?). Now, there's a whole book to be written about negative self-talk and stopping it (*makes a note*) [*Stop making notes for new books, Rob – Ed.*], so I'll keep it brief here. When you notice you're saying negative things in your head (or out loud, if that's how you roll) about yourself, your work, your body, your actions, your creative outputs, stop. Stop that voice. Tell it off. 'Don't talk about me that way!' Now say something nice to yourself, as if you're your best friend. It might feel awkward and even embarrassing at first, but keep at it – it'll make you feel more confident.

The same goes for what you say to other people about yourself. That doesn't mean you have to go around telling everyone you're the dog's bollocks (for my American friends, that means 'really great') – no one likes an arrogant arse ('ass' for you). You don't have to stop with the self-deprecation either – it's funny, relatable and can be a great way to connect with people. But if you're constantly negative about yourself in front of other people, if you're always pointing out your own flaws and short-comings and failures, not only will you begin to make them question why they're hanging around with you, but you'll also dissolve whatever confidence you have. Find a balance – still be a bit funny, don't take yourself too seriously, own your mistakes and be confident and positive about yourself when it's appropriate. And if someone compliments you, say THANK YOU.

2 Try things that make you grow or challenge you

We've looked at this in detail already, so I'll summarize: get out of your comfort zone and take a risk.

3 Try to master something

If you're like most entrepreneurs, you're a master of being a jack-of-all-trades – a generalist. You're good enough at loads of things across the business, probably because you had to do everything at the beginning. I think this is a great thing, and it can open you up to many more possibilities than specializing in one field. But the downside is you can miss out on the really exciting feeling that comes with mastery.

There's an idea that, if you're the master of one thing, you're the master of everything. This idea comes from Japan – hundreds of years ago, monks would focus intensely on a problem for days, giving every fibre of their being to solving it. Focusing on solving a tiny problem – such as 'What is the sound of one hand clapping?' – gave them the tools to master anything. By mastering something, you're equipping yourself with knowledge about how to learn (which, as we've seen, gets you prepared for opportunity). It also shows you that you can be great at something, which boosts your confidence.

4 Honour all the things you've done or are great at already

When did you last really appreciate the fact that you're really good at cooking? Or that you can play the piano? Or whistle through your fingers? (How do you do that?!) You are already brilliant at something – what is it? Honour it. Spend time doing it, enjoy the feeling you get by being really great at something. Enjoy the feeling of flow, enjoy the time slipping past you. Smile, be mindful of what you're doing.

Sometimes we forget what we're good at, and just by remembering, practising the skill, letting our confidence shine through, we invite new opportunities.

5 Review what you do well and what you fail at doing

Now you've taken the time to honour what you've mastered, think about all the things you do in your life, work, hobbies. What do you do well? What do you do not so well? What do you completely suck at?

A lot of people will tell you to work on your weaknesses, but I think that's completely wrong. Work on your strengths and ditch your weaknesses. (There is a caveat here: some weaknesses you will need to work on – the ones that would otherwise get in your way. You need to make that call.) Life's too short to invest time in something that's unnecessary. If you're a fashion designer who's terrible with spreadsheets, get someone else to do your finances and spend your time designing clothes instead. I don't mean quit everything that's a bit hard (I'm assuming you've read this section up until now) – you need to challenge yourself. But if you're spending loads of time doing something that's not a strength, that wouldn't be beneficial to you to develop and that you don't enjoy, find a way to stop doing it. You'll be happier, you'll be more confident, you'll invite more opportunities.

By getting out of your comfort zone and doing something new, you can kick-start this great cycle – the more confident you are, the more you'll try, the more opportunities will arise, the more you'll do, the more confident you'll become and so on. What are you going to try first?

Summary

We all have our comfort zones but, if you stay in yours, new opportunities aren't going to start flying around you. To be prepared for opportunity, you need to take risks and challenge yourself. Get out of your comfort zone and you'll get more confident and start to see how shiny new things, places and people can open the door to opportunity.

TAKE ACTION

You guessed it: *get out of your comfort zone!*

What one thing can you do right now that makes you feel uncomfortable? Can you pick up the phone to a potential partner? Book a flight and go somewhere new for the weekend on your own? Apply for a new job or sign up for a course?

Do it! Take the first step, and bask in the warmth of your newfound confidence.

12

Use your mistakes and problems

I've just told you that one way to be more confident is to review the things you're good at and your failures. But I didn't tell you what to do with those failures. Don't throw them all out, bury them or burn them so you don't have to face them ever again (I know that's what you're thinking). There's a much better way to use them.

I'm sure you know this. But do you act on it?

When I asked my social media communities about their definition of opportunity, one of the biggest themes that came out was failure: people talked about getting opportunities as a result of mistakes and failures, about using problems to open opportunities. They talked about seeing the upside in mistakes and failure. This is huge, and it's something you need to start doing if you want to invite opportunity into your life.

There are some really well-known stories. Thomas Edison invented the first commercially practical light bulb, but he failed 10,000 times before that. J. K. Rowling is the world's first billionaire author (I'm working on being the second), but 12 publishers rejected Harry Potter before that.

One story I really like is about the Mars rovers. Down here on Earth we watched rover after rover break down and fail. We got excited and then disappointed as NASA announced one failure after the other. Then the rather brilliantly named *Opportunity* landed on Mars. *Opportunity* ended up being the longest-serving rover of them all, providing evidence of water and potential life on Mars.

What all these stories have in common is persistence in the face of failure, and applying the lessons from mistakes to go in new directions. It's not about blindly kicking a ball, hoping it'll land in the net, and doing the same thing over and over again, only to hit the goalpost. It's about taking the feedback from the mistake and stepping a metre to the left or changing your angle. It's about being flexible and using that mistake.

Look for the challenge

Mistakes feel bad. Failure feels bad. It fills us with shame and makes us want to hide. If you've failed or you're facing a problem, you probably want some comfort, some sympathy, some support. Many people end up playing the victim, because it's easier than being active and embracing the challenge. Most people, when they're faced with a problem, will say 'Why me? Why now? Oh, I can't afford it. This always happens to me …'

The stupid thing is that when people swim in their problem like this, they get consumed by it, they drown, whereas if they saw it as a challenge and tried to solve it, they would be able to take control of it. Having a solution-focused mindset is essential in business, and I think it's massively valuable in every area of your life. Look for the challenge in the problem, search for the solution. Let the opportunity appear.

I interviewed Marc Randolph, who was the first CEO of Netflix, for my podcast. He believes that you have to be a filter to problems, but you can't get sucked into them. If you look at the world, he said, take a sceptical or even pessimistic perspective so you can look at everything as a problem. Once you see the problems in everything, you can then start to come up with the solutions – create the upside, release the opportunity. He believes that entrepreneurship and success and growth and progress are all about finding the solution to a problem.

'You've got to train yourself to look for pain,' he said. 'To see the world as an imperfect place. And once you've recognized how flawed the world is, all of a sudden ideas almost instantaneously flood in. You start by saying "what's frustrating to me?" And you almost can't help it. You get this "what would happen if …?" that pops into your head.'

I interviewed billionaire entrepreneur David McCourt on my podcast, too, and he went as far as to say the world's biggest problems can all be opportunities.

'The business opportunity is solving the environmental problem. The business opportunity is solving the educational problem. To say that there are 4 billion people in the world that don't have high-speed internet, that's not a political problem, it's a business opportunity. To say that there are a billion people without clean water, that's not a political problem, that's an opportunity. To say that education in America, where the price is going up 8 or 9 times faster than wages, that's a business opportunity.'

(Both Marc and David said loads of other brilliant stuff. If you haven't heard them yet, check out their interviews on my podcast – www.robmoore.com/podcast)

OK, so you need to get excited about problems – yours, other people's, the world's. Seeing the problems puts you at risk of being consumed by them, but you can't do that. You have to focus on the solution, you have to see the problem, understand it, then step back quickly and address it.

Entrepreneurs have this mindset. Investors have this mindset. Coders and hackers have this mindset. Notice the problem, acknowledge it as an opportunity to come up with a solution, then take that opportunity and come up with the solution.

Think about it, you can't imagine a coder who's about to start a big project suddenly spots a problem and gets consumed by it and says, 'Oh f★★★ it, I can't be arsed to code today.' They're much more likely to see a problem (the bigger the better), roll up their sleeves, order a pizza and pull an all-nighter, smiling in the glow of thousands of lines of code on the screen.

Be that coder. Embrace the problem and look for a solution.

Turning your own problems into opportunities

I want to say from the outset that I don't think anyone should be going out trying to make mistakes and failing and having problems. I hear a lot of people giving advice that you should make mistakes so you can learn from them. That's dangerous advice. What if those mistakes are real mistakes that you can't bounce back from? What if you ended up losing your business in a recession, or getting a divorce, or losing your house because you couldn't afford the payments?

A friend of mine is the poster boy for this. In the 1980s, Gerald Ratner was the head of Ratners Group (now Signet Jewellers Limited) – a jewellery company with a turnover in the billions. He was hugely successful, he had swagger and he was bold. His confidence and entrepreneurial mindset saw him push the company from strength to strength, making high-profile acquisitions and massive returns for investors. It also made for great after-dinner speeches, and he was invited to speak frequently.

One day in 1991, he spoke at a conference being run by the Institute of Directors. He made a joke in his speech: 'We also do cut-glass sherry decanters complete with six glasses on a silver-plated tray that your butler can serve you drinks on, all for £4.95. People say, "How can you sell this for such a low price?" I say, "Because it's total crap."'

The company's value sank by £500 million *overnight*.

Did Gerald learn from his mistake? You bet. Would he do it again? Hell, no.

Why make all the mistakes yourself? One mistake could ruin you! Some mistakes aren't necessary. The lessons you get from them aren't worth the negative results. I think the best way to get the same experience is to learn vicariously through other people's mistakes.

This is one of the benefits of expanding your network and putting yourself out there more – you get exposed to more mistakes you can learn from. You can turn other people's failures and problems into opportunities for you. Ask people about their mistakes and what they learned. Build a knowledge base of other people's mistakes and prepare yourself so you don't have to make them yourself.

I think recessions are a great time to learn from other people's mistakes and invite opportunities. In the last big global recession in around 2008, my business was probably still too small to fail and be really damaged by the recession – we had fewer than 50 properties and five staff at the time. We had been semi-stalking some big players in the property industry in the UK and, when the recession hit, two big businesses went bust. Bad news for them, but we saw an opportunity to learn.

We had lunch with these big players every few months, we would ask them for advice, and they took us under their wings. We kept a good relationship throughout the recession, and it meant we had front-row seats to what they went through, their challenges – like being too scared to reduce the size of their team, how quickly they had to make decisions, managing cashflow (coping with less than one month of cashflow in the bank rather than 24–36 months').

We learned so much from them. That knowledge has helped me see opportunities I wouldn't otherwise have had, because I haven't been through that failure, I haven't personally faced those challenges.

Here are three ways to get opportunities from other people's mistakes, failures and problems, without having to suffer them yourself:

1 Get mentors. I've said it before and I'll say it again, mentors are amazing, and they'll take you to the next level in any area of your life. Grill them about their failures and how they overcame challenges.
2 Network. The more people you meet, the more mistakes you'll be exposed to. Ask them for their top tips and advice. Ask what they learned in their worst moments. But be gentle – you don't want to reduce people to tears in the middle of an event by picking at a fresh scab.

3 Read. Did I mention it's good to read? People who have survived massive hardship often write autobiographies – find them and devour them. (Gerald's autobiography is a great example – *Gerald Ratner: The Rise and Fall and Rise Again*, as is the book we wrote together, *Reinvent Yourself*.)

One really incredible example of someone who turned their own challenges (which seems like a massive understatement) into opportunity is the Pakistani human rights activist Malala Yousafzai. As a young girl, she was prevented from attending school when the Taliban took over her town. She was shot in the head by an extremist after speaking out in support of girls' education – and she survived. After being brought to the UK for treatment, she recovered and used her experience as an opportunity to support girls' education globally by co-founding the Malala Fund. In 2014, she became the youngest person to win the Nobel Peace Prize. She was 17.

To me, this is absolutely incredible. Thankfully, most of us will never have to endure what Malala did and, put in her situation, even the strongest of people might have been broken down, unable to see any kind of light, let alone turn their plight around and have an enormous positive impact on the world.

There's a real mindset aspect to this. Back in Part 1, we looked at some research into luck. One of the other findings was that 'lucky' people handle adversity differently from others. In particular, they can see the upside to their problems, they don't dwell on their problems, and they take action to find solutions. Importantly, they also believe that they will be successful – they believe that everything will turn out well in the future.

Some might say this is blind optimism, but there's evidence that it has a real impact on the outcome. Imagine this: you've got partial facial paralysis because of complications during birth, you went through the foster care system, you were unemployed and homeless, and you even had to give up your dog because you couldn't afford to feed him. What would you do? Would you maintain hope and follow your dreams?

Well I, for one, am glad he did: this is Sylvester Stallone.

He knew he wanted to be an actor but, because of his facial paralysis, nobody would cast him. At his lowest point, after sleeping rough at a bus station in New York, he sold his dog to a stranger outside a liquor store for $25, crying as he walked away.

But he knew what his future could hold. He wrote *Rocky* and tried to sell the screenplay. He was offered $125,000, but he turned it down because they refused his request to star in the movie. Then he turned down an offer for $250,000, then $350,000. Eventually, the studio agreed to cast him, but they cut the offer by 90 per cent. He walked away with $35,000 and the role that would change his life forever. The first thing he did was buy back his dog ... for $15,000!

I hardly need to tell you this, but today Stallone is one of the world's most successful actors. The *Rocky* movies amassed ten Oscar nominations and three wins.

Thousands of actors have learned from Stallone's hardships and challenges, just like thousands of writers have learned from J. K. Rowling. They are inspiration to be persistent, not give up, keep pushing and stay optimistic about the future. Only then will you be creating the conditions for opportunity to swoop in and help you out.

If I look at my own life, I've made loads of mistakes, just like everyone has. I don't regret anything, but there are certainly things I'd do differently. I wouldn't go to uni, for example. But even then, I learned things from my university experience that I might not have done otherwise – I learned that I definitely didn't want to be an architect. That you can't learn to be an entrepreneur at university. That I don't need certificates to be successful.

Mistakes lead to successes. Problems lead to solutions. Challenges lead to triumphs. You just have to take a step back, turn them around and look at them with a positive eye.

Summary

If you have the right mindset, you can turn your mistakes, failures and problems into opportunities. There are countless examples of people throughout history who have turned negatives into positives, from Thomas Edison to J. K. Rowling to Malala Yousafzai. But you don't have to get the experience directly; in fact, mistakes can be dangerous. Try to get the lessons without the risk – learn from other people's mistakes by talking to them, seeking mentors and reading books.

TAKE ACTION
. . . .

Write down one mistake, one failure and one problem you've experienced in the last month.

How could you turn them into opportunities? Take a step back and consider:

- What can I learn from this?
- How can I turn it around to my advantage or to help someone else?
- What solution could I come up with?

Choose one of these and take a step towards the opportunity. That could be by writing a blog post about your experience or talking to a potential partner to help you develop your solution, for example.

PART 3
How to seize opportunities

13
Opportunity

Deal with it

'If a window of opportunity appears, don't pull down
the shade.'

Tom Peters

Now that you've laid a strong foundation – you've learned knowledge in Part 1 and prepared yourself in Part 2 – it's time to skill up
and start dealing with opportunities.

There is one last thing to do before you get stuck in, and that's
open your mind.

There's a lovely little saying that I really like: the mind is like a
parachute – it works best when open. A lot of people are closed-
minded: 'Oh, there's no opportunity here. Oh, there's nothing to
see here. Oh, it never works. Oh, I always fail. Oh, people always
want to screw me over. Oh … blah blah blah.' They're expert
at seeing all the negative things happening to them and around
them, but they don't see opportunity at all. They just focus on the
negative, on the downside to every situation.

I think being open-minded is seeing the upside potential in
everything. Seeing the upside potential in people that you meet,
even if you think you don't have much in common. Seeing the
upside potential in an idea that someone's pitching to you, even
if you're a little bit cautious about it. Seeing the upside in the
problem and deciding to see the challenge as an opportunity.

Think about some of the really well-known examples of
serendipity.

Penicillin

Alexander Fleming didn't bother cleaning up his lab properly before going off on holiday for a fortnight in 1928. When he got back, he noticed that the mould that had contaminated a petri dish growing bacteria had killed that bacteria. He investigated and discovered that the mould produced penicillin, which has since been used as an antibiotic, saving millions of lives.

Corn flakes

In the late 1800s, the Kellogg brothers John and Will were busy coming up with the blandest foods imaginable, with the aim of dulling people's 'passions'. Food to stop you f***ing. They left some cooked wheat out and rushed to treat their patients, and by the time they returned, it had gone stale. Bingo! Corn flakes.

Post-it notes

The creation of the Post-it is basically a collection of accidents that people noticed and saw as opportunities. First, 3M scientist Spencer Silver accidentally made a 'low-tack' glue when he was trying to develop something really sticky. He tried and failed to pitch the product for years, until a colleague, Art Fry, used it to stick his bookmark in his hymn book. The trademark yellow? Another accident – it was the only colour paper the lab next to the Post-it developers had at the time.

Open minds

What all these things have in common is people with open minds. Fleming was open-minded enough to notice something others wouldn't have seen. The Kelloggs were open-minded enough to taste something others would have thrown away. Silver was open-minded enough to see an opportunity in his failure and Fry to see a use for it.

Being open-minded isn't just about welcoming surprises in your environment and through your actions. Even more than that, it's about how you connect with other people. Being open-minded is about being optimistic, being enthusiastic, being passionate. It's about charisma. It's about being in flow. It's about having a high energy and a high vibration, so that when people come into contact with you, they feed off your positive energy.

When you spend time with people who lift you up, they make you feel good. You stand taller when you're around them. I think that's what being open-minded is – it's looking for solutions in everything, learning from everyone, not glossing over anything, paying attention, being ready to be proven wrong.

Why am I making this point now? I think in the last few years, the world has got a bit more closed-minded. Whatever your political leaning (that's one of the few topics I won't touch with a barge pole), it's clear that we're divided. People are polarized and they don't want to hear anyone else's opinions. We've built brilliantly effective echo chambers on social media and in real life, so all we're exposed to is confirmation of our own beliefs. If someone questions something, rocks the boat, suggests a different perspective? NO! TROLL!

The result is people who don't listen, people who won't change their minds, and people who limit their own opportunities.

Don't be like that. Don't limit your opportunities by closing your mind.

So right now, now that you've learned about opportunity and are prepared to welcome it, take the time to open your mind. Decide right now to be less judgemental, more flexible, more interested. Choose right now to get rid of your echo chamber and look at everything afresh. Start right now to question your assumptions and look at things from new perspectives.

Are you ready to be open-minded? Then read on.

How do I handle opportunities?

After all that preparation, we're getting to the juicy bit: what you actually do with opportunities.

As I've already said, I think this can be broken down into three stages:

1 Spot the opportunity.
2 Assess the opportunity.
3 Take the opportunity.

In the next three chapters, we'll walk through the skills you need in each of these areas to maximize the opportunities that are right for you, at the right time. I'll share my own experiences, a few stories from other people and loads of practical tips.

This will work best if you're ready to work on your opportunities as you read: following the tips in this part of the book, you'll be able to identify an opportunity (or two, or three, or hundreds), assess it and take it – or not. You've hopefully been taking action since the start and, by now, you might have a notebook half-filled already. Look back over what you've written. Keep thinking about your situation, what opportunities you have, what you've been missing. This will help open your mind and get you into the opportunity groove.

Summary

You've learned about opportunity, you've created the conditions to let it happen, now it's time to open your mind. Being open to opportunities is the last thing you need to do before you can start spotting them. When you're ready to see things in new ways, be proven wrong and look at things from new perspectives, you're ready to seize opportunities.

TAKE ACTION
· ·
Switch off your assumptions.

We all make judgements and assumptions to make it through life; there would be too much to process without them. But now I want you to switch them off.

What assumptions are you making that you could stop, step back from and think about differently? Are you assuming you can't do something? That someone can't help you? That something is out of your reach?

Choose one assumption and switch it off. What opportunities pop up without that barrier?

Do this as many times as you like – the more you do it, the more you'll build up a picture of what's possible if you keep an open mind.

14
Spot the opportunity

It's time to find your opportunities!

But what do they look like? Where will they be? And when will they appear?

That depends on you. What's an opportunity for one person might not be for the next. It depends on your personality, your skills, knowledge and experience, your areas of expertise, your interests and passions, your location and mobility, your flexibility, your goals and desires, and many other things.

I'm going to go through 11 approaches that will help you spot opportunities. As you go through them, write down opportunities that you notice you have now or could prepare for. Your list will hopefully grow until you have loads at the end of this chapter.

1 Recognize an opportunity

At this identification stage, I think it's best to consider every opportunity a good one. What you're doing is collecting them. It's like collecting all the oysters first and then checking them for pearls after. What you're looking for are the oysters. With that in mind, an opportunity could be pretty much anything.

It might be a big-hitter – a job vacancy, a marriage proposal, a potential investment, a business idea ... Or maybe it's small – a free weekend away, a talk at an event, a window of time in your day to have an uninterrupted bath with a glass of wine and a good book.

It might be fast – a competition that's closing soon, a house that's on the market in a popular area, a business that's about to be liquidated. Or maybe it's slow – a new relationship, a new direction in your career, a manager who's planning to retire in a year.

It might be easy to spot – do you want your dream house at a cut price? Do you want your dream job? Do you want to go to Fiji without paying a penny? Or more difficult – do you want to commit to a 12-month fitness programme? A new life in a new country? A baby?

These are all opportunities; some will be right for you, some not, but at this stage you can't discount anything. As you collect more and more opportunities, you'll become more and more of an expert. You'll learn to recognize them fast.

2 Give it time

When you plant a seed, you don't come back the next day and shout 'Where's my f★★★ing tree?!'

You've prepared, but that doesn't mean opportunities will flood in right away. If there's one thing you're hoping for in particular – meeting someone special or making millions or landing your dream job – it's unlikely to fall in your lap as soon as you close this book. Be patient. Wait. (Use the time to get bored!) Remember the opportunity you want to invite, visualize what it might be like, revisit the idea every now and then, but don't let it close you off to other things.

It's highly unlikely that you're setting up for one opportunity at a time, so make sure you keep your horizons broad. Of course, you need persistence and focus; you might need to be relentless if you want a publishing deal or investment for your business idea. But make sure you keep back some time and energy for other things.

This is one reason I think it's a great idea to keep notes. Write down opportunities you want to have and go back to your list every so often. What you don't want to do is forget what you're looking for and then miss it when it arrives down the line.

3 Expect the unexpected

But just in case, have a failsafe for if that happens. Always put contingency planning in place for things you didn't expect. Leave space for things you didn't expect. I use the 70–20–10 model: in business that means I spend 70 per cent of my time and energy on the big, income-generating work, 20 per cent for the thing I'm developing and 10 per cent for the mad new ideas.

It's a great model you can apply to every area of your life. The 70 per cent is your main dish – the big project, the thing you have to focus on to get the best result. Maybe the 70 per cent is a painting you're working on. Maybe it's the biggest or most important room you're decorating. Maybe it's volunteering for the local scout club.

The 20 per cent, then, is the smaller, newer, more fun thing you're doing. It's the side dish – the thing you're testing out or building up. Maybe you're a pianist who also plays the violin. Maybe you're a translator who works in English and French and you're learning Mandarin. Or maybe you've just started a shop on Etsy to sell your handmade photo frames alongside your corporate job.

The 10 per cent is where you leave room for the unexpected. It's a sandbox, a place to play. It's where you can go with the things you didn't see coming, like the idea for a new business that might be crazy.

To expect the unexpected, you can train yourself to look for patterns – try to predict things you wouldn't ordinarily have seen coming. Imagine you walk the dog every day. You take the same route at the same time, you bump into the same people and have the same conversations. You start paying more attention and you notice that one of the people you see but never speak to always has a coffee cup from a café down the road. That's a pattern. If you hadn't spotted that, you might have been surprised to see that person in that café and you might not have been prepared to talk to them, ask them out and eventually marry them. (Or you might have ended up like me, fumbling around for something charming to say, and eventually wearing down the love of your life until she marries you.)

4 Use your imagination

When was the last time you really unleashed your imagination and thought like a kid? When you threw away all the rules and regulations you think exist in the world and got imaginative? Forget gravity, let's float. Don't worry about language – let's imagine everyone can understand each other. Ignore ageing – we can choose to get older or younger at the flick of a switch.

This is all absurd (unless you've got an idea for the last one … I'd love to get a bit more of my hair back!), but it's a great exercise to challenge rules and see *what if*:

- What if you didn't have to live where you do?
- What if you were so wealthy money was no longer an issue?
- What if you could speak that language, play that sport, fly that plane?

Your imagination is incredibly powerful. You can use it to literally make things up – take something that exists and reshape it into something new. Look at a product you use and think about how you could change it to make it better (or even worse), or how you could use it for a different purpose.

I'll save you a bit of time here: knives make lousy screwdrivers, you can make a pretty decent medieval castle out of a clothes rack and a sheet, and the sofa is never, ever as comfortable as the bed, even if you were right (this is an official apology to my wife in advance for anything I might say or do that would get me sent to the sofa again).

5 Keep track and learn

I've mentioned keeping notes about your opportunities, but I think it deserves more attention here. When you're as prepared as you are, you'll be batting opportunities around all over the place, and it'll difficult to keep up with them all. Write them down. Include details – what the opportunity is, where it came from, when it appeared – and revisit, updating them when something changes. Set reminders to go back to things, call people, take action. (I've got some great tips for doing that in Part 4.)

When you keep track of things, you can learn much more from your experiences. You'll notice your own habits and patterns. The opportunities you play down and the ones you blow up, the opportunities that make you scared and the ones that make you excited. Learning about how you deal with opportunities also teaches you about you, how you function, what you like and don't like, where you excel and where you fail. All that information will feed into your decision-making process when you assess and take decisions.

6 Be a trend spotter

Some people seem to have a crystal ball. Take Gary Vaynerchuk. He's the CEO of VaynerMedia, a YouTube star, a multi-bestselling author and a massively successful investor. A big chunk of his estimated $160 million net worth came from some really smart investments he made early on in brands that became dominant. Twitter, Tumblr, Uber, Snap, Coinbase.

It seems like he somehow knew what was going to hit the big time. Of course, he says that's not the case – his secret is to invest in things he likes and understands, then to ride the wave and not expect a quick pay-out. Wise words indeed.

I think there's more than a little trend spotting at play. Experts say this kind of skill is partly down to something called 'perceptual acuity'. Perceptual acuity is the ability to see round corners or over the horizon. To see how things will change and understand that environment. People who develop their perceptual acuity can make decisions for a business that propel it forward when others stay static, choose investments that seem risky for others but that end up giving a high return, be first to jump on the next big thing that actually does become the next big thing.

Barry Cunningham. Brian Epstein. Peter Thiel. What did these people have in common? High perceptual acuity – they took an early leap by publishing the first Harry Potter book, giving the Beatles their first record deal and being the first person to invest in Facebook.

You can do the same. You can identify seeds that might grow into the next innovative idea. You can be a trend spotter while everyone else is stuck in today's world. Here are a few ways to do that:

1 Learn about your business niche or area of interest. Talk to more people, read, stay up-to-date with news. Set time aside every week to top up your information.
2 Watch while people take risks and follow the results. Try to spot patterns and see if you can make predictions. Like 'fantasy football' for opportunities.
3 Look at things from a new perspective. TikTok might not have seemed like a safe bet to you at the age of 40, but imagine being a teenager and look at it again. Change your perspective and look at the world with fresh eyes – you'll learn something new every time.

7 Tinker

One great way to spot opportunities is to tinker with what's already in front of you. If you're in business, you might make little changes to products. Combine services in new ways. Adjust something to make it serve a different audience.

I think this one is really closely related to an approach we'll come back to in Part 5: Start now, get perfect later. When you have an idea or see a potential opportunity, you can uncover the real opportunity by launching it, doing it, getting it out there, and then tinkering with it while it's live. With feedback from people, and results at every step, you'll adjust in a way that brings the opportunity to the top.

I do this with my Make Cash Challenge. In the challenge, people have to make as much money – cash in the bank, not invoices – as they possibly can within a certain number of days. When I launched it, it was really a prototype – a pretty good one, but still incomplete. I knew it was a great idea and an opportunity to support my community. People loved it and made thousands over six days. I listened to their feedback, heard their requests and tinkered with the design. I tried six, seven and eight days. I developed the guidance I gave out with it. I changed the support I was offering – the live videos and posts – and encouraged people to connect to the community more.

The results prove that tinkering works. It turned what looked like it might be a great opportunity into something that's actually changing people's businesses and lives. On average, the people who have taken part have made about £5,000, with the reigning winner raking in £37,000 – in a week!

8 Look for ways to help others (and yourself)

Problems and challenges are opportunities; you can spot opportunities by understanding people's problems and needs and paying attention to the things that bug you. A bride's frustration with planning her wedding resulted in the massive wedding website The Knot, which 80 per cent of couples planning a wedding in the USA visit today. A woman's frustration that she couldn't find underwear that would be invisible under her white trousers resulted in the billion-dollar clothing company Spanx. Two friends' frustration with the lack of electronic invitations resulted in Evite – and for co-founder Selina Tobaccowala, a series of high-profile corporate positions at Ticketmaster and SurveyMonkey, and another start-up called Gixo.

These frustrations are everywhere. It might seem like there's an app for everything these days, but life is constantly changing, and so are its problems. What are people struggling with? How can you help them? In the business sense, where can you add value?

A great way to do this is to understand and look to create fair exchange. Some people call this win-win, but I think fair exchange is more elegant, more accurate and probably a little bit deeper. Fair exchange is the sweet spot, the optimum elasticity of price and value, whereby the producer and the consumer, or the two recipients of the exchange, get maximum benefit. When you create fair exchange, whether it's at work or at home or in some other area, you all of a sudden attract a lot of opportunity, which you can then spot.

Let's look at a commercial transaction to see that in action. Fair exchange is where the producer gets the maximum profit margin, without it turning into greed or power, and the consumer gets the maximum value for the transaction. When it swings too far in one direction or the other, it's no longer fair exchange. On one side, a bargain is where the consumer gets more than they perceive that they paid for, and they would feel happy and grateful that they got good value. That may not be fair for the producer, who may not be able to make a margin, so it may be unsustainable. But then go too far the other way and you've got something that's overpriced or undervalued, which is unfair in favour of the producer, so the consumer would feel ripped off.

Now this is completely elastic in every market, in every product, in every life situation. It's an ever-moving target and it changes with trends and with evolution. Think about when things come out: at first, they're very expensive, then they become commoditized and then they become free. Take Wi-Fi for example – you always had to pay for Wi-Fi, and now it's mostly free in the UK. At the other end, there's now paid content like Netflix, Facebook supporter programmes and online courses. These are things we might have expected free in a different format, but that are now providing so much value we're willing to pay for them.

You can see fair exchange in other areas, too. Fair exchange in a partnership is where one partner goes out and builds the empire and the other partner supports the building of the empire in terms of looking after the children and managing the home and serving and supporting the person going out and building the empire. One person brings certain values and skills, and the other person brings different values and skills.

Now, by the way, it doesn't always have to be fair; you can attract opportunity by giving the other person an unfair exchange in favour of the other person. In dating, you might pay the full bill at the restaurant. But watch out – if you make unfair exchange a habit, even if it's tipped in the other person's favour, you can end up creating a problem. So the sweet spot, the equilibrium of opportunity, is fair exchange.

If you want to increase your fees, if you want to increase your value, if you want to have better negotiation, position and power, then create more value.

It's certainly true that the more value you create, the more opportunities you get, the more clients, the more followers, the more gratitude, the more people who are fans of your work, the more good opportunities that you compound and bring into your life.

A lot of people struggle with fair exchange by making it *unfair* exchange, either through greed and power and selfishness, or too much selflessness – letting other people encroach on their time and giving everything away for free. When it's the latter, they often do that through a fear of judgement or ridicule or criticism. So the maximum opportunity that you create in your life is that equilibrium of fair exchange. Look for fair exchange and you'll find opportunity.

9 Be prepared to work for it

As I explained in Part 1, luck and serendipity don't just happen. People talk about manifesting and the law of least effort, and I'm all for trying things like that, but you need to do more than sit back and wait. You need to do more than imagine and wish. Everything you want in life won't just fall in your lap without you lifting a finger.

Sure, go ahead and set your intentions, goals and vision, focus on your outcomes and put good vibes out there. You should be doing all that. But you have to seek out your serendipity – you have to go out into the world and find your opportunities.

That takes work. You've already done a ton of work in getting prepared to invite opportunities, but I'm afraid it doesn't stop there. You have to be active if you want to spot opportunities.

Remember being a kid and searching for conkers? You don't just stand there and look around where everyone else is, where they're all smashed and mushed on the ground. You have to get down on the ground and search through the leaves. You have to look where no one else is looking.

When you're spotting opportunities, you need to put the work in and take the untrodden path. Look in unexpected places that take you out of your comfort zone and require effort.

10 Don't go it alone

Yes, you have to work, but you don't have to take on all the burden yourself. Why not build a team that can find opportunities for you? As you've probably gathered, I think you can get way more out of life by leveraging the shit out of it, and the same applies to spotting opportunities.

Put together an opportunity team. That might be people to take tasks off your hands and free up time for you to get bored (cleaner, driver), people to bounce ideas around with (partner, friend), people to ask for advice (mentors, coaches), and people to do the legwork, scour the industry and keep you updated with potential opportunities (your employees).

Keep your team open – you might find support in the most surprising places. Remember Barry Cunningham, who I mentioned earlier? He's the publisher at Bloomsbury who said yes to Harry Potter. Well he didn't do this alone: he asked his expert – his eight-year-old daughter Alice – for her opinion on a sample of the book and she advised him it was an opportunity he shouldn't pass up. (In not so many words anyway – she demanded the rest of the book.)

11 Don't ask, don't get

This is a big one. I believe there's an infinite number of opportunities that are on the table, you just have to ask for them. My dad always, always, always said to me, 'You don't ask, son, you don't get.' And yet I hardly asked for anything until I was about 26. I spent most of my life worrying about what people would think of me, and there are so many things that I could have done in my life but didn't do, just because I didn't ask. Sometimes the opportunity was right there on the table, and I didn't ask.

When I finally opened my eyes and realized I wouldn't go up in a puff of smoke by asking for something, I found out that there were women who liked me, too; I'd never dated them, because I didn't ask. I found out that there were business opportunities out there and partnerships that I could have made, but I didn't ask.

My podcast has now passed 400 episodes. I want to interview some of the most inspiring, amazing, biggest guests in the world. I sometimes worry that they're too big and famous for me, and I get that fear of asking. I sometimes have connections who know brilliant guests, but I don't want to ask for an introduction because I don't want my connections to feel like I only want them for their connections. This goes around in my head because I'm a bit soft. Aren't we all sometimes?

But the cold, hard truth is that if you don't ask, you don't get. I started putting this to the test. I posted a request on my Facebook page, saying 'I'd love to interview Billy Monger. I watched his documentary, it was so inspiring. Does anyone know him?' It just so happened that his cousin follows me and sent me a message with his mobile number. I froze. What the hell am I going to say? 'Hi, Billy Whiz, I'm such a big fan, I think you're inspiring, will you go on my podcast, pretty please?' (How's that for a bit of imposter syndrome?) So I asked for an introduction, and he put us in touch on WhatsApp.

I did the same with Tess Daly, who co-hosts the BBC hit show *Strictly Come Dancing*. I'm friends with one of the professional dancers on the show, Kevin Clifton, and he's taken me backstage a couple of times. I bumped into Tess (cue goggle-eyed schoolboy impression) and I was blown away when she said she followed me. Tess Daly! Follows me! I really wanted to contact her to invite her for an interview, but I didn't want to ask Kevin in case he thought I was using him for his connection. But you know what? Don't ask, don't get. I left him a message live in front of an audience... I'm still waiting (hoping, praying, rain dancing, ha-ha).

I think we're all relatively good at asking for things we're confident in. The challenge is asking for things you're not yet confident in. I'm really good at asking for what I want in business generally, from my team. I'm also good at asking for help in an area I'm not considered an expert – I can put my hands up and say, 'Hey, you know I'm a newbie, can you help me?' The interesting thing I've learned about myself is that it's in between those two things – in areas where people think I'm an expert but I'm not yet 100 per cent confident – that I'm afraid to ask for help in case people judge me.

What will they think of me? What if I'm embarrassed? What if I fail? What if they think I'm lame and stop following me?

Tell that annoying voice to shut up, and just f★★★ing ask. Hold your breath, grit your teeth, pinch your arm, however you want to get through it, just do it.

There's this great little thing that someone told me about years ago: the three second rule. Nope, it's not how long can you leave a chip on the floor and still be socially acceptable if you eat it (that's five seconds). It's when you want to ask for something, and you know that it's something that you want to go for, you've got to do it within three seconds. Hit the send button. Go up and speak to that person. Get that selfie with your hero.

Any longer than three seconds, and you'll talk yourself out of it – your brain will find all the reasons why you shouldn't ask. I wouldn't be married to an amazing woman today if I hadn't asked within three seconds. When I saw my now wife (then 'hot blonde') walking across the bar, I recognized her from the gym. I just held my breath and went up and talked to her.

Does it get easier? Sometimes. Is it ever really easy? No. Asking for things is uncomfortable and difficult. But I've pulled myself together and made a commitment to ask even more. Will you?

Summary

You've learned that opportunity is everywhere, you've prepared yourself for it and now it's time to spot it! There are 11 great ways to spot opportunities: recognize an opportunity, give it time, expect the unexpected, use your imagination, keep track and learn, be a trend spotter, tinker, look for ways to help others, be prepared to work for it, don't go it alone, and don't ask don't get.

TAKE ACTION
. . . .
Spot opportunities.

Try at least three of these methods for spotting opportunities and write down as many as you can find. For each one, take note of:

- what the opportunity is
- where you spotted it
- who (if anyone) it's connected to
- one thing you would need to make it happen.

15
Assess the opportunity

By now you're probably swimming in opportunities – a whole heap of rocks with a few diamonds hidden in between.

Now you have to start sorting through them, assessing each one and deciding whether it's right for you, right now.

First, get the easy ones out of the way. Are there any you are absolutely certain you want to take? Any you're certain you don't want to take? Maybe you've done your research, weighed up the opportunity before it appeared. It could be something you'd been waiting for, or something you'd been considering. If that's the case, go ahead and make a decision – I'll outline how in Chapter 16.

For everything else, which I'm guessing is most of the opportunities you've spotted, you'll need to do some kind of assessment to figure out if each opportunity is right for you, and right for you right now.

I don't think there's a hard-and-fast way to do this – I think each opportunity probably needs its own approach to figuring out its merits and coming to a decision. But there's a handful of things I tend to do when an opportunity comes up that I don't instinctively know what to do about.

I'll go through those things here. Ready to go through an assessment with one of your opportunities? Choose one that came up in the previous chapter, run it through each of the assessments and see what comes out the other end.

Ready? Let's go.

Due diligence

You want to create, not just more opportunity, but the right opportunity. To do this, you need to do some quality research and due diligence. We've covered a lot in this book, including the abundance of opportunity and the limitless nature of the opportunity, but sometimes too many opportunities can be overwhelming. What you've got to do is disqualify opportunities as well as qualify them.

This is where good research, background checks and due diligence come in – whether it's for business, a new house, a school that you might want to put your kids into, or even a romantic partner. When you're doing due diligence and research, your goal is to *disqualify* more than *qualify*. It is to be sceptical rather than optimistic, to try to find out what could go wrong in the future.

1 What do you already know? You'd be surprised by how much you know. Write notes about everything you can think of – add to the skeleton you started in the previous chapter and flesh it out. Think about background, history, your own connection to the opportunity. If it's a new job, what do you know about the company, the people working there, the position, the prospects and so on? If it's a new house, what do you know about the area, the local schools and hospitals, the house itself?

2 Who is involved? Write down all the people who have a stake in the opportunity. Note any 'red flags' – people you don't know, don't trust or don't like.

3 What can you find out about the field, industry or area the opportunity sits in? Now it's time to start researching. Google is the best starting point – start searching for information that can add to your knowledge. Then look to other sources – people you can ask, print archives you can visit, places you can go to gather information.

4 Most importantly, eventually stop researching. Put a limit on this process. You could probably go on for ever, and

research has a tendency to turn into active procrastination. Don't let it become a barrier to taking the opportunity – you'll be shooting yourself in the foot!

5 If you feel there are gaps you want to fill, go back to one or two sources and get that information.

When you've got the full picture, ask yourself how you feel about the opportunity. Is it something that would work for you now? Do you feel confident in taking it or not taking it?

Assessing risks

Anyone in business will know about risk assessment. It comes from the business world, but I think it works for every part of life. When you do a risk assessment, you think of all the risks – all the things that could go wrong, all the things that could be dangerous, all the things that could be a total disaster – and score them. You then make plans and put processes in place to prevent them from happening and to limit the damage if they do.

Let's use a restaurant as an example. You might identify risks like a step up to a raised platform (risk of customers and staff tripping), an unstable tree leaning over the building (risk of losing the roof ... and cracking a few heads), a fire (the chef likes to flambé), loss of staff to a new restaurant (you've heard rumours that something might open next door), and so on.

Then you go through each risk, work out how likely and how risky it is (tripping on a step isn't as bad as a tree crashing through the roof) and give it some kind of score. Then you come up with solutions: what can you do to prevent the risk? Maybe you can strap the tree up or turn the step into a slope. And finally, you plan for the worst: what will you do if the tree does come crashing down? What processes can you put in place to evacuate people if a fire breaks out?

You can apply this risk assessment process to any opportunity. Let's look at a new business. Imagine you have the opportunity to open a gym. Now you'd need to do a full risk assessment of a gym, of course, but that's not what this is about. Here you're doing a risk assessment of the *opportunity*.

Risk: The business fails, and you lose your investment.
Likelihood and seriousness: It's a new business, so that's an inherent risk. But your research suggests there will be demand, you're an expert in the area and you have a partner who is just as invested as you. It's a huge risk (10), but it's not very likely (3).
Prevention: Work with your customers to develop exactly what they want. Make sure your income is diversified – offer personal training sessions and rent out office space for other businesses above the gym.
Worst case: You could get a loan or further investment to cover losses if it's feasible to grow; you could cut your losses and kiss your investment goodbye.

Risk: Your partner quits and leaves you hanging.
Likelihood and seriousness: You met them at a networking event and they seem cool, but you're not long-time buddies. It's not a huge risk because you could run it yourself if you needed to (4) but you have to assume it might happen (5).
Prevention: You could have a partnership agreement or contract in place that outlines a commitment from both of you, with a get-out clause that wouldn't leave your business hanging.
Worst case: Your partner leaves and you burn out and end up having to sell or pass on the business. You could identify a shortlist of backup partners in case this happens and have an exit strategy to make sure you get your investment back.

This is just a made up example, and you might go through a whole load of other risks – the more risks you identify, the better. Your goal is to see all the risks, assess them and mitigate them.

Since we're searching for problems, I also want to mention a process that the US entrepreneur and podcaster Tim Ferris talks about called 'fear setting', which is the opposite of goal setting. Rather than setting out ambitious goals with the aim of meeting them and getting a positive outcome, in fear setting, you literally imagine the worst possible outcomes. You set out your fears – the potential disasters that could happen if you take an opportunity – and you assess the opportunities on that basis.

The great thing is that, psychologically, if you've already played out your worst fear in your head, you've disarmed it. You've tasted the failure and realized it's not deadly. You've faced the demon and now you're ready to move on and leave at least some of your fear behind.

Do keep a little bit of fear, though. It'll keep you on your toes. The moment you stop seeing the potential dangers, risks and downsides is the moment you're really at risk. And remember, you do have to take risks (I'll say it again: if you don't risk anything, you risk everything). Take them with your eyes open and you'll be much more successful.

Return on investment

Another concept borrowed from business is return on investment (ROI). This is a pretty straightforward idea: how much are you investing, how much will you get back and what's the difference? If you're investing more than you're getting back, it might not be a great opportunity. But maybe that doesn't matter to you. You have to assess ROI in context.

Traditionally, this is about money. If you're investing $100 and getting $200 back, that's a great return on your investment. If you're investing $100 and getting $10 back, that's not so good. It's the basic measure investors use to inform their decisions.

But what if one or both sides of the equation don't involve money?

Imagine you're investing $150 in a workshop to learn to quilt. Your return on the investment is a skill. How can you measure that? One way is to think about how that skill could play out in the long term. Do you plan to sell quilts? Or teach other people? You can start to put dollar amounts on those things (tentatively) and then see if it makes sense.

Imagine you're investing three months in writing a novel. You're planning to set up a Kickstarter campaign to fund it, and you're aiming for $5,000. That won't cover your salary for three months as well as the editing, printing and distribution of the novel. Are you happy with that? Will the happiness, satisfaction and pride of publishing a book make up for the shortfall?

Imagine you're struggling to have a baby and you've decided to try IVF with your partner. It will cost $50,000 and the chance of it working is about 10 per cent. You could end up with no return, or with the baby you've always dreamed of.

On the surface, ROI is simple, but as soon as you apply it to opportunities in different areas of your life, you see that it's complex and really personal to you. This kind of assessment takes deep thinking, and while you're the person who will really understand the value of both sides of the equation, you might want to find someone to bounce ideas around with.

Asking for advice

Proceed at your own risk. It seems like everyone has an opinion, like everyone is ready to give you advice (often when you haven't asked for it). Some of the people waiting to share their thoughts about your opportunity will be worth listening to. They'll have more expertise than you, or more experience. They'll be wise or smart or intuitive. But for every person who's worth listening to, there are a thousand who need to shut up.

Here's what I think you should do (because I'm one of the people worth listening to, ha-ha): decide who you want advice and input from and go and ask them directly. Block out anything else that comes in.

Getting outside perspectives is really important, because they'll hold up an opportunity at a different angle to you, they'll see it in a different light – in the context of their own lives and experiences and thought processes. That's what you need if you want to get the full picture before you make a decision.

What you don't want is a whole wave of half-baked advice from people who have no idea what they're talking about. It'll literally drown you. You have to learn to spot and take the useful advice and ditch the rest.

That's a really great skill to develop, because it allows you to go out and crowdsource ideas and feedback, then filter through it and pick out what's helpful. Now I don't mean only the good stuff – you don't want to play to your biases and only listen to the people who agree with you, far from it. But you also don't need to listen to the pointless negativity that comes from some people – the criticism for the sake of it rather than the constructive input.

I mentioned The Knot earlier – it's a US-based wedding website that 1.8 million couples visit every year – that's pretty impressive considering there are 2 million marriage licences granted in the USA each year. In an interview with Quartz, Carley Roney, one of the co-founders (the other being her husband, David Liu), said one of the company's biggest successes had been down to them ignoring people's advice. When they started throwing the name around and asking people informally for their opinions, the reviews were mixed: people weren't totally on board with 'The Knot' (people had an issue with the silent 'k'). Their investors, AOL, all but demanded they change the name to 'Weddings Online' (inspired, don't you think?). But Roney dug her heels in – and it paid off. 'This quirky name, with all its faults, could have been the death of us in a search and data-driven world, but it is considered by many to be one of the secrets to our success,' she said. 'It worked.'

Sometimes you have to trust your instinct, just like Roney did. Ask for advice and be open-minded about what comes back. But don't follow it blindly.

And remember, you can also feed off of other people's experience and advice by getting mentors, asking great questions at events and reading books. Someone has always been there, in some shape or form. Find that person and grill them.

Timing is everything

In business, an estimated 90 per cent of start-ups fail. In his 2015 TED Talk, which has 7.5 million views, serial entrepreneur Bill Gross revealed the biggest factor in the success of start-ups. He studied the idea, the team, the business model, the funding and the timing and looked at how these five factors played out across five top companies that all hit $1 billion, and five that failed.

The results were really interesting. It wasn't the idea that came out on top. It turns out it's the timing that's the most important factor in a company's success. He talks about two companies in particular: Airbnb was perfectly timed because it was set up at the height of the recession when people needed extra money; same thing for Uber – drivers signed up because they needed more money.

'The best way to really assess timing is to really look at whether consumers are really ready for what you have to offer them,' Gross said in his TED Talk. 'And to be really, really honest about it, not be in denial about any results that you see, because if you have something you love, you want to push it forward, but you have to be very, very honest about that factor on timing.'

Look at your opportunity as if it's a start-up (that's easy if it actually is one). Be brutally honest with yourself. Is the timing right? Is it right for you? For the world? Would it be better to take the opportunity in a month or a year or five years? Is that possible, or is it now or never? And if it's now or never, can you make changes to make the timing fit?

Let's say someone noticed one of your sculptures at a gallery and you have the opportunity to do an art residency for a month.

It's your dream opportunity … but it starts in two weeks and you're meant to be moving house. The timing sucks. Can you move the residency? Can you change the date of your move? Can you ask someone to take on the task of moving? Or is everything so un-shiftable that you have to say 'no' to the opportunity?

Now think about a business opportunity. You have the opportunity to invest in a really exciting virtual reality start-up. You're sure it's the future but you think it might be a bit early. It's a lot of money and you need a new car. The timing isn't great. Does the start-up need your investment right now? Will you miss out if you don't get in there on this round? Do you really need the new car, or can you use public transport, borrow a car or do a car share for a while?

There's no formula to figuring out if the timing of an opportunity is right. I can't give you a simple equation that spits out a 'yes' or 'no'. You need to weigh up the pros and cons and decide how much of a risk you're willing to take. Sometimes it'll be obvious one way or the other, but it's often not so simple. For those opportunities, you need to hone your gut instinct – and you do that by practising, testing and learning along the way.

Does it suit you?

One of the biggest factors that will determine just how much of a risk you're willing to take is how well the opportunity suits you.

This is where the work you did in Part 2 comes in. You got to know yourself, which means you're now probably better at knowing if an opportunity lines up with what you love, value, obsess over. These things evolve too, of course, but does the opportunity fit with you now? Do you think it might in the future?

When you're assessing opportunities to see if they're a good fit with you and your life, I think it's good to think in a few different directions:

- What do you love? What are you really passionate about? What gives you a warm fuzzy feeling when you think about it?
- What do you need? What would improve your life right now? What's missing?
- What do you value? Everyone has different values, and the more an opportunity lines up with yours, the more likely you'll be to take it.
- What makes you money? Some people say money won't buy you happiness, but I disagree – money has changed my life in so many positive ways, and it can do the same for you. Will the opportunity help elevate your wealth?
- How does it compare to the equivalent happening in my life? This is something people neglect because it's dull. The shiny new thing is exciting, right? But think about what you're already doing or have done in the past that's similar to the opportunity and ask yourself if you would be better off focusing the extra effort, time or money on that.

Going through these questions should help you figure out how well the opportunity fits you and your life right now. If everything's lining up, it's time to take the next step.

Do a test

They say opportunity comes disguised as hard work but, as you've probably gathered by now, I think opportunity comes disguised in challenges and in problems. The initial opportunity can be different from the actual opportunity; the opportunity that you're looking for might be two or three or four stages or iterations or pivots away from the current opportunity. It's almost like the Russian doll effect – an opportunity hidden in layers of decoys.

You often won't realize it, and it won't become clear until you try it. So, having a testing mentality, having a 'screw it, let's do it' or a 'f★★★ it, just try it' mentality is really good for creating opportunity. Most products nowadays are version 512 – pretty different from the initial product. But that rarely means drastic change; it happens in small steps. After more than half a century, Porsche's design language is still very similar to the original concepts, and its changes are evolutionary rather than revolutionary. You see the same everywhere – we get software updates on phones and other devices on a weekly basis, getting rid of little bugs and giving us slightly new functionality.

I think we can apply this testing mentality to taking action on all sorts of opportunities. My business partner, Mark, and I have a lot of partnerships. In the very early days, we'd probably just go into the partnership a bit blind, but as time went on we would try to negotiate out a partnership. Both of those approaches can cause problems later. I think that the ideal balance for forging or creating or moving into a new opportunity is somewhere in the middle of going in blind and doing all the diligence, research and negotiation upfront: to do a test.

Let's say you want to do a joint venture with someone to buy a house with them – they put the money in, you source the property. You could do one as a test. You could arrange it so that you both have ownership, the person who funds it has the security or the charge, but you don't necessarily have a full-on joint-venture agreement or long-term contractual relationship. You just buy one deal and see how it goes.

That's how Mark and I have bought hundreds of properties together – by trying one deal and seeing how it went and then deciding if we wanted to do another one after that. We're currently doing a few joint-venture arrangements, and they're all progressing differently. We've been negotiating on one of them for about nine months. On another one, we're still going back and forth over the structure of the earning after nearly a year. But for the third one, we decided to agree on a simple revenue split and try it for six months. That one has had much less friction to getting started, and much more flexibility in continuing; in six months, we'll probably be doing things slightly differently from how we initially envisaged it. Later down the line, we can decide whether we want a proper structural joint-venture arrangement.

This kind of approach doesn't just work within a single opportunity, it can change a whole company. Royal Dutch Shell is one of the oldest examples – now an energy giant, it initially started as a small antiques shop in London, selling imported shells. The company took a small step at a time, expanding its import and export business until it had enough ships that could support its move into the oil industry in the late 1800s. It's now a giant in the petroleum industry and, as far as I know, has no small antiques shops to its name.

Nokia went from paper mill to mobile phone manufacturer. Nintendo went from making card games to computer games; Coca-Cola from producing medicine to beverages; Rolls-Royce from planes to cars.

The great thing about having a testing mentality and the flexibility to change is that you're constantly discovering. You have an open-minded, inquisitive, curious nature, and you end up stumbling upon new ways of doing things, rather than holding onto the old ways. That means you can evolve with the trends, you can grow, you can be organic and fluid and you can have the variety that you may crave.

There are a few simple rules to making a testing mentality work for assessing opportunities:

1 Make sure you're testing it the right way

If you're thinking about launching a product, can you prototype it? If you want to change a service, can you test the new format on a small group of people? If you're considering moving to a new country, can you go on holiday there first? Think bitesize.

2 Have a plan

Yes, I think you should jump in. Yes, start now and get perfect later. But don't go in blind – have a plan for what you want to test, how you want to test it, what you're going to measure and what the results will tell you.

3 Test, assess, adjust, test, assess ...

Commit to a few rounds of testing – if your opportunity is the tiny doll surrounded by five others, you need to give yourself a fighting chance of getting to the middle. Test your opportunity and measure the results. Weigh them up, consider them, decide whether they can feed back into the test. Run a second round and do the same.

4 Know when to stop

At some point you have to make a decision. That decision could be to run with the opportunity on an ongoing test basis – it works for our joint-venture property deals. But if it's a 'yes' or 'no' decision that needs to be made, draw a line and give yourself a clear point at which you decide.

Prioritizing

Life isn't linear, and neither are opportunities. You won't get a steady stream of one after the other, coming at the right time and never interfering with the other things going on in your life. It doesn't work like that. If it did, no one would need my books. (Phew.)

Opportunities are messy. They come along when you least expect it and force you into difficult situations. They make you choose when you'd rather not. They have absolutely no f***ing respect for your plans or processes.

Isn't that exciting?! Variety is the spice of life, right? Except for when you're overwhelmed, drowning in work and responsibilities and deadlines and problems, only to be totally thrown by a whole load of new possibilities.

There's a simple way to deal with overwhelm – including when opportunities are the issue: prioritization. I won't go into detail here, because you'll find a summary of my approach in Part 4 (and masses of detail in *Life Leverage*). For the purposes of assessing opportunities, you need to see where they fit in your overall life, by prioritizing things.

What would happen if you slot the new opportunity into the rest? What would drop off the end? Are you OK with that?

You could also use prioritization as a way of assessing opportunities against each other. This could be a really simple process: take a stack of serendipitous Post-it notes and, on each one, write down an opportunity you have right now. Arrange them in a line, from worst to best. Now throw away the worst half of them. What you're left with are the better opportunities, which you can look at against the rest of your life and work. Can you fit them in? Can they be priorities in your life? Should they be?

By doing this, you'll have a chance to uncover some of those hidden diamonds. Comparing opportunities side by side will help you spot the ones that are special, the ones that are head and shoulders above the rest – the stars. Those are special. Those deserve your attention. Those are the ones you need to look at more closely, test out and start now (get perfect later).

Future-proofing

If you're unsure whether to take an opportunity, fast-forward five or ten years. What would a proud, successful, balanced 'future you' perceive of you deciding to take this opportunity or not? Would they be pleased that you took that decision?

For example, many of us have been in relationships that we've stayed in for many years, knowing in our hearts that it's not right, but not having the strength or the courage to make the decision to end it. Perhaps that's due to fearing the consequences or the embarrassment of the split, or worrying about how it may affect our children or our partner, or not believing that we can handle being alone. But what would our future self say if we came out of a really traumatic or difficult or wrong relationship? They would say 'I'm proud of you. Good on you for being strong.'

I always like to think about what my future self would say to me about an opportunity I'm weighing up, and what they'd think about how I handled the process of assessing and taking the opportunity. And if I decide that future me would be proud or feel like the decision was a good one, then it's probably the right decision for me now.

Summary

When you've spotted an opportunity, you need to work out if it's a good one – for you, now. There are several ways you can assess an opportunity, and you can mix and match these approaches depending on what it is: due diligence, assessing risks, return on investment, asking for advice, timing is everything, does it suit you?, do a test, prioritizing and future-proofing. After assessing your opportunity, you'll be ready to make a decision.

TAKE ACTION
. . . .
Choose one of the opportunities you spotted in the previous chapter and run it through one or more of the assessments. Did it help? If it did, would another one add more value? Do that. If it didn't, which would be better? Do that. Try out a few approaches and get comfortable with assessing your opportunities out in the open.

16

Take the opportunity

You've prepared, you've spotted opportunities and you've assessed them. Now it's crunch time: you have to make a decision.

When it's easy, revel in the certainty. Enjoy shouting a big fat 'YES!' or a loud 'NO!' Move forward with it or throw it out of your mind.

Taking opportunities (or not) is rarely that simple, though. So in this chapter, we'll look at some of the things you might come up against at this stage, and what to do once you've said 'yes'.

Making fast decisions

There's a big difference between making fast decisions and having to make fast decisions because they need to be fast. Sometimes people make decisions too quickly; I've done that once or twice (or a thousand times). When you do have more time to do research, take the time to analyse the opportunity as much as you need to. But when there's a time crunch, you need to be prepared to get stuck in and take a leap, to a certain extent. This could just be an opportune moment, a trend. It could be the competitors are all over it or someone's given you a very specific and hard deadline.

Here are some ways to make fast decisions:

1 *Always be ready to make fast decisions.* Make sure your diary is flexible and you can move and delete things quickly if you need to. It's about prioritizing: if you need to make a fast decision about an opportunity, that opportunity needs to take priority.

2 *Learn to do fast research.* Hit fast-forward on the assessment process in the previous chapter. Take shortcuts, ask for help.

3 *Set yourself a deadline.* If you haven't been given one, set yourself one. It will focus your efforts on making the decision; without this, you'll stumble around for weeks or months or years, thinking it over. (We had a hard deadline recently, and it was so hard, Mark called me when I was on stage speaking to 500 people – and made me talk to him!)

4 *Learn to trust your intuition.* You need to be self-aware here – if there's evidence that your intuition can't be trusted, reach out to people who are better at this and ask for their advice.

5 *Test fast.* Again, run through the process of putting the opportunity to the test, but at warp speed. There's a great book called *Sprint*, by Jake Knapp, formerly of Google Ventures, that outlines how to test an idea in five days.

6 *Go into obsession mode.* Shut everything else out – turn off smartphones and laptops, silence messages and calls and emails, and spend five or six hours of a whole day thinking and obsessing and researching and discussing and evaluating and allowing yourself to go around the houses a few times on the decision. By doing that you're effectively concentrating a much longer process.

7 *Tweak the opportunity.* Can you compromise temporarily? Start small? Bring someone else in to share the risk? If there are small changes you can make to the opportunity to make a fast decision easier, do it.

I love a good bit of rallying, especially when I'm up against a tight deadline. As soon as we had the opportunity to buy the promotion company and we'd made the decision to go for it, I basically dropped everything I was doing and went into full obsession mode. We got the deal done at lightning speed – it was probably a few days, but it felt like hours – and in that time we did everything we could to get them everything they needed. From that point it moved very quickly. And that was one of the finer asset purchases that we've made.

Making big decisions

Right now, especially in business and on social media, speed is vital – your competitors can get out there with a new product or service in a matter of hours, so the pressure's on. But, of course, sometimes when you've got big decisions that impact people and their livelihoods and their employment, you have to evaluate all the situations and you have to take much slower thought processes. You can start to activate your slow, logic-based thinking and rely less on your more instinctive, emotion-based fast thinking.

Every decision will have different elements and for big decisions, if they're big and they need to be fast, you can follow the steps in the previous section. If you've got more time, you can start to appreciate the gravity of the opportunity a bit more.

When you've got time, you can do research, carry out due diligence, ask people's opinions, meditate on it, take time to walk and get a clear head, evaluate all the different scenarios and situations. It would be wise to do that if your once-in-a-lifetime opportunity doesn't need to be rushed.

Sometimes people think all opportunities are once-in-a-lifetime opportunities. When people are selling you something or they have a fear of missing out or they get excited very easily, they're quick to declare, 'Oh, it's a once-in-a-lifetime opportunity!' Are they? Usually not.

I think you have to really understand what the opportunity is to you and how frequently it's likely to come up for you. The more infrequently it comes up, the more seriously you've got to take it; the more frequently it comes up, the more you may need to tone down your excitement and fear of missing out.

Here are the practical steps you might take with a big decision:

1. Rearrange your routines and priorities

If you've got a life-changing opportunity, you need to be able to clear your diary, to change your routine, to go to a different time zone, to completely cancel plans and make new ones.

2. Be prepared for pain

People probably assume that a once-in-a-lifetime opportunity is a positive one, but it could equally be something negative. It could be the hardest decision you have to make in your whole life. It could be the breakdown of a relationship, the winding down of a company, the relocation of a family. Take the time to feel strong, because you'll need that emotional strength to take a big negative opportunity.

3. Put the decision into perspective

Is it one giant all-consuming opportunity? Or could you see it as a series of smaller ones? It's like eating an elephant – you do it one bite at a time. (I recommend that you do not attempt to eat an actual elephant.) By breaking the opportunity down into smaller pieces, you're making the huge, scary decision into a series of smaller ones – you're not scaling a cliff edge, you're walking up a staircase.

Start with 'no'

Right off the bat, I'm going to start with something that's really trendy: saying 'no'.

Did you just shudder? Nobody likes to say 'no'. It's a trait many entrepreneurs share – me included. When I interviewed David McCourt for my podcast, he shared that he finds it hard to say 'no'.

But 'no' is so important – it's the only way you can stay focused, keep your strategy on track and succeed. Saying 'yes' to everything creates overwhelm, stress and tension, which lead to procrastination and inaction. If you want to use opportunities to help you seize the day and win at life, you have to suck it up and get tough. Make 'no' your best friend.

Saying 'no' is hard, especially if you have shiny penny syndrome and you get off on starting new tasks, new projects, new businesses, new relationships. But 'no' is what gives you self-respect. It's about having boundaries that are solid, even to you, and especially to other people.

Just think about what would happen if you said 'yes' to every opportunity.

You'd be ecstatic ... for about half a day. Then the pressure would set in. You'd start panicking, your heart rate would increase along with your caffeine intake and you'd miss a deadline ... two ... three. You would try to work faster and start making mistakes; the quality of your work would plummet. You'd miss family dinners, fun days out and, eventually, Christmas. While you steadily built up an angry resentment, seasoned with guilt and stress, everyone around you would start to see you as unreliable, scattered, shaky.

Sounds great! Where do I sign up?

Seriously, though, even knowing all that, we're still prone to agree to things because 'no' is so hard to say. Saying 'no' is the new big thing, so if you google it, you'll come up with a whole load of advice and tips. I don't think it's good to focus on either side of the coin; I also didn't love the *Yes Man* obsession a few years ago, after Danny Wallace spent a year saying 'yes' to everything and wowed the world with his hilarious stories. It's another paradox: you can't say 'no' all the time and you can't say 'yes' all the time.

In my book *I'm Worth More*, I outline some ways to say 'no' more easily:

- Say 'Yes, but not now' or 'Yes, but we can do it later or schedule it in once I am done?'
- Say 'So-and-so can help you better with this, why not ask them?'
- Never answer the phone or respond to an email unless you are free and not in the middle of something important. Call or email them back when it's a good time for you.
- Have a gatekeeper – a PA, VA or message filter – that only lets the messages you want reach you directly.
- Schedule specific times for specific tasks like meetings, calls, admin and giving back.

I'm much more likely to say 'yes, but not now' than I am to say 'no'. That's because I get excited by new things, I want to squeeze every drop of opportunity out of this life and I don't like to close doors. Saying 'yes, but not now' is like leaving the door on the latch – I know I can always go and open it later when I'm ready.

I've done this in many different areas. I decided years ago to create a book writing course and a LinkedIn course – I have the expertise and interest in those areas. But the timing hasn't been right, so instead of saying 'no' to those opportunities, I say 'yes, in three months', and I'll keep saying that until it's the right time. Same goes for books – I've got maybe 15 book ideas in Evernote, all waiting with a 'yes, but not now' keeping them in the app. And for years I've wanted to take Progressive to the global stage, to run events in as many countries as we can and serve the world. But that would mean less time with my family, and I'm not ready to be away from them like that. So it's a 'yes, but not now'.

I also believe that the world reacts to how you teach it to behave towards you. Part of embracing opportunities is about retraining that behaviour by turning down the opportunities you don't want and saying a big 'YES!' to the ones that are perfect for you.

There's another way – for opportunities you think are great and want someone else to benefit from, you can pass them on. Flip forward to later in this chapter to read more.

Say 'HELL, YES!'

'If someone offers you an amazing opportunity but you are not sure you can do it, say yes – then learn how to do it later!'

Richard Branson

If it's not 'no' (or some form of 'no'). then it's 'HELL, YES!'

What now?

You've got work to do. When you've decided to take an opportunity, you don't have to jump in with both feet. You can dip in a toe first, then one foot, then take time to get used to the water. By breaking in slowly, you're limiting the instant impact the opportunity has on your life and, instead, giving yourself the chance to adjust.

Mark and I have nine streams of income. Nine. Did we start that in one go? Absolutely not! It's taken us 12 years to build up to nine streams of income. We leveraged existing income streams to add on new, related income streams. The more thinly you're spread, the less time you can put into each stream, and the more time wastage there is jumping from one to another.

If you jump in with both feet, you might end up drowning, then you're faced with that crippling overwhelm and procrastination that happens when you say 'yes' too much.

Let's imagine you see an opportunity to quit your job and you jump right in and just jack it in. You've seized that opportunity and you've made a decisive move. But now you have no income, no buffer, no gentle slide into a new reality. And before you know it, you're rifling through supermarket bins for a just-within-date microwave meal.

OK, I'm being extreme, but you get the picture.

Instead of jumping in, you could reduce the days you worked at that job and start increasing some other kind of work or source of income.

On the other hand, sometimes hedging your bets can be the wrong way to take an opportunity – it can be better just to go for it. I've heard plenty of people say that when they held on to their comfort blanket of a nine-to-five salary they never pushed themselves to succeed as an entrepreneur, and that it was being made redundant (or sacked, like me) that gave them the shove they needed.

One other point to make here is that when you're getting started with a new opportunity you've decided to take, you almost certainly don't have to do it alone. You could form a joint venture or partnership, ask for help or advice from mentors or coaches, talk to your family and friends. Spread the love, share the pressure.

Overcome obstacles to starting

You're about to jump in, and then BANG! Your inner voice screams 'WAIT!' Out comes imposter syndrome, fear of failure, overwhelm. You've researched the hell out of the opportunity, and you know it's right for you, right now. You've made the decision to take it ('HELL, YES!'), so why are you suddenly holding yourself back?

When Dima Ghawi got married and moved from Amman in Jordan to San Diego in the USA, she thought she would discover her identity and be respected for who she was. But, in reality, the opportunity turned out to be very different: she was expected to do more to maintain a perfect image, to serve her husband and his family; she was hardly allowed to talk to her own family. She was trapped.

Scared to stay in the relationship but terrified to leave, Ghawi felt she had nothing to live for – and she wasn't even 25 years old.

One day, she decided to feel the fear and take action anyway – she left the marriage.

Her family disowned her, and her own father tried to have her killed to save the family's honour. The only way she knew to move forward was with education. She enrolled at the University of San Diego and started to study. A year later, she wanted to practise her interview skills, so she applied for a number of jobs … She got an offer from every single one, and she accepted an offer from IBM.

'I was so terrified … of leaving San Diego, of leaving the past behind. Terrified of proving myself in this big company,' she said in her TEDx talk.

'But the same intuition kept telling me, feel the fear and take action anyway. And I did. And that's when the world opened up for me. I got to work and travel around the world with IBM. I lived in Japan for over a year. I got to work on projects with them at the United Nations, in South Africa. I got to lead global teams. And every day I would wake up and remind myself to feel the fear and take action anyway.'

I love to challenge myself to do things that I initially feel fear around. With a few caveats aside (if I'm not acting unethically or aggressively, hurting people or doing something illegal), if I feel like I should do something and I worry about it I will just dare myself to do it, I will take that risk. If I feel like I should say something, but I worry about being brutally honest, I take the chance and say it anyway. If I'm on stage giving a speech and I think of a good comeback or joke, but it could be risky, I'll just say it (again as long as it doesn't offend, upset or shame someone). And they always land brilliantly! Lead balloons have great landings too, you know.

My whole life I've been good at art. I always enjoyed it, it was a passion of mine, and I could draw for hours or even days without anyone motivating me. I never did anything with it, but it was always there. After my architecture degree, I was working in my parents' pub. I had zero desire to do architecture, I don't know why I did the degree, but I went back to the pub because Mum had said Dad wasn't very well and asked me to help out for a while. I was considering going to Australia to be an architect (bloody glad I didn't do that in the end!) and I thought why not, I'll help out for a few weeks.

Four years later, there I was, still working in the pub, living someone else's journey and walking their path instead of taking my own. I felt very suppressed, a little bit bitter and pretty lost. I knew that I didn't want to work in the pub long term, and I think my parents knew that, too. But they wanted to help me, and I felt some moral obligation to help with the family because of my dad's illness. But it wasn't just that; I didn't know what else to do, I was scared, and I got myself stuck.

Then one day, my dad and I had a massive argument behind the bar. We shouted and screamed and effed and blinded at each other, and he kicked a huge box full of 32 bags of crisps right at me and it hit me, in front of 60 customers. I shouted, 'You can go f★★★ yourself and stick your job right up where the sun don't shine!' and he shouted, 'Good, get the f★★★ out, you're not working here again!' I love my dad, and we didn't argue very much, but when we did, that was how we argued.

I walked away, panicking, thinking, 'OMG, what am I going to do with my life?' I lived next door at the time, literally ten metres away. I walked out the pub and into my house, and in the ten seconds that took, I had decided I was going to be an artist. I made the decision, and that was it. Maybe I didn't have any other opportunities, maybe I didn't have any other skills, but the bridge had been burned. I had to face my fear and try to find my own path.

I didn't succeed or thrive as an artist, but fast-forward a few years and it got me into working for myself, it got me independent. Art turned out to be the bridge between failing at working in a pub in my mid-twenties and building a successful property and business empire with my business partner, Mark Homer. Had I let fear delay or prevent me from making that decision, had I stopped to think of all the (probably valid) reasons not to be an artist, I wouldn't be where I am today. That scary, fast decision was one of the best ones I've ever made.

Pay it forward

I want to end this chapter on a really important note. Some opportunities that aren't right for you might be perfect for someone else. If something exciting comes up but you can't run with it – maybe the timing is off, or you have other priorities – then paying it forward can give you massively positive returns.

Virtually all of your opportunities will come through people. So doing good, supporting people where you can and lifting them up will help you get more of what you want or need. Leveraging partnerships to create goodwill, using the law of reciprocity, creating friendships and connections and shared time and history and experience and emotion – this will all help you get more opportunities through other people.

I truly believe that, if you help others, they will help you. If you help people get what they want, you will get what you want. If you build up goodwill in the proverbial bank by doing good things for people without expecting anything in return – you do it because you want to help them and not because you want something back – paradoxically, you'll probably get more back.

Help as many people as you can. Be kind to people. Do good things for people. Try to do this every day, and you'll build up a massive amount of light and goodwill that will return the favour and give you limitless and abundant opportunities.

Your positive actions could be in the form of gifts, solutions, partnerships, collaborations, introductions to people, lovers, houses to buy. They could be in the form of opportunities.

Try being an opportunity broker. The next time you spot an opportunity that's not for you, before you say 'no', take a moment to think about who it might be for. Your friend? Colleague? Neighbour? Sister? Father? Point it in their direction – don't say 'no', say 'yes, but not me'. Do this as much as you can and see the positive effects on your life and the lives of the people around you.

Summary

Make fast decisions and big decisions, start with 'no' and say 'HELL, YES!' Overcome obstacles and pay it forward. Once you've assessed your opportunity, you need to make a decision, and then follow through on it. Face your fear – sometimes the best decisions you'll ever make are the scariest ones. Pay attention to the true nature of the opportunity and treat it carefully. You don't want to drop it after all the work you've put in.

TAKE ACTION
. . . .
Sort your opportunities.

Choose three of the opportunities you've identified in this section – one 'yes', one 'no' and one 'not sure'.

1 For the 'not sure', make a fast decision. How did it feel? Do you trust your intuition? What would make you feel better about it?
2 For the 'yes', start slowly – find a way to ease yourself into it. What could you do to soften the transition?
3 For the 'no', think of someone you know who would benefit from the opportunity and pass it on to them. How did it feel?

PART 4

How to seize the day

17
Get practical

This book is called *Opportunity: Seize the day. Win at life.*

I wanted to show right there on the cover that winning at life is the accumulation of a million tiny actions, a million decisions, a million opportunities taken on a micro level. It's like the pixels that make up the image on your computer screen. The atoms that make up the book (or Kindle or smartphone …) you're holding.

All you can do is win the day. You win at life by winning more days than you lose. By having more good days than bad ones.

I'm very lucky to be living in the UK, where the average life expectancy is 81. If I live to 81, I will have lived 29,586 days. That's 29,586 chances to seize the day, 29,586 chances to make good decisions and accumulate those small wins into a life that I want. Time is finite. We can't manage it, but we can decide what we do with it.

Of course, there's a paradox here. If you focus on the minute detail, on the day-to-day, on the tiny wins, you risk losing the bigger picture. If you focus only on the day, if you keep your eyes low and don't look far into the future, you risk forgetting that you still have 15,000 days left to win. You need a goal; you need a roadmap or a plan. But that journey is made up of millions of footsteps.

This doesn't just count for seizing the day; it's also the way we self-destruct. One person who explains this really well is Lisa Nichols. She's an American entrepreneur who is CEO of one of the world's biggest training and development companies, Motivating the Masses, but she hasn't always been on a winning streak.

Twenty years ago, Nichols was a single mother on benefits with $12 in her bank account; it was a whole series of little decisions that got her there. She didn't make a big decision to be abused, but a small decision to lower her integrity bar. A small decision to stay the first time. A small decision to accept his words to make up for his behaviour.

Then one day she stepped back and saw the life these little decisions had been leading towards. 'It's never too late to hit reset and fall madly in love with the life you've been given,' she said. She believes you have to get to know yourself (tick!) and love yourself before you can make a change. Because opportunity is inside you, and it will show itself only if you let it.

When I look back at my years working at my parents' pub and my time as a skint artist, I see a long series of days when I hid the opportunities inside me by covering them with self-loathing and self-doubt. Days of getting by, of being cynical and closed-minded. Days of making the wrong decisions – because doing nothing to change is also a decision.

I let my life become menial instead of meaningful.

Turning it around is hard, but it's not a mountain you have to peak in one massive jump. You climb, one step at a time. You use ropes and harnesses and a helmet. You surround yourself with support and prepare for failure.

There are loads of metaphors here: Rome wasn't built in a day. You don't eat an elephant in one bite (again, put the knife and fork down). The reason it's so ingrained in our clichés and idioms is because it's true: we live one day at a time, and that's the only way you can win at life – by seizing the day.

Part 4 is all about that. It's full of actionable, practical tips, lots of them from my previous books. Each chapter is short and sweet, so you can take the framework and apply it right away.

But now, turn to a new page in your notebook or document and get ready to write.

Summary

You don't win at life in one go; you do it day after day after day. If you want a successful life, you have to seize the day – Part 4 will be all about how to do that.

TAKE ACTION

. . . .

Chunk an opportunity.

Think about an opportunity in your life that seems overwhelming, too huge to handle. How could you break that down into day-sized chunks you can seize more easily?

18

Start the night before

My day started last night.

Before I went to bed (and I went to bed early – I'm not one of these robots who can function on four hours of sleep a night … and neither are you, by the way), I prepared for what was going to be in front of me when I woke up.

If you want to seize the day, being prepared will give you a head start. There's no way of knowing exactly what you'll face, but if you know exactly what you want to achieve, you'll be well on your way to marking that day off as a win.

When the kids are in bed, I go through emails and messages and send some replies. I find after six o'clock in the evening is the best time to do that, because you won't get caught in a game of email tennis at that time – a lot of the people you're in touch with will have left work for the day and won't get back to any messages until the morning.

I then spend time reflecting on the day I'm closing off, thinking about what went well and not so well, and what I can do the next day to make sure it's a win.

Then it's time to write a list. Now I don't call it my 'to do' list, I start with 'to leverage' – you'll find out more about this in Chapter 22 on LMD. I write a list of the things that need to be sent out for other people to do, and I make sure I send instructions to people before they get to work, so they can start their day well, too.

Then we might get jiggy (I'm sure my wife won't mind me sharing with you that the best time to do that is 19:45–20:15 – it's permanently BLOCKED in my diary), and I'll wind down and get some sleep. I sleep really well after that last appointment.

Plan for opportunity

When you're planning the next day, think about opportunity. What can you do tomorrow to prepare for opportunity, to create the conditions to make it happen, to spot or assess or take an opportunity?

1 Think about all the opportunities you've got right now – go back to your notes on the Take Action task from Chapter 14 on spotting opportunities if you need a refresher. Which of them can you do something about tomorrow? Is there some research you need to do, a decision you need to make, an opportunity you want to pass on to someone else?

2 Write down a task on your list. If it's an important opportunity, put that task right at the top. That's the most important position on the list – as you'll see soon, I think you should obsess about ticking this item off, not just ticking items off in general.

3 Now think about what you can do to create the conditions for opportunity to happen. Is there something from your list you can do tomorrow? (Remember: get to know yourself, put yourself out there, find the balance, fill up your brain … and empty it, step outside your comfort zone and use your mistakes.) Maybe you could read a couple of chapters of a book or write a blog post about something that went wrong today. Write the task on your list.

Make this a recurring habit – on your daily list, include one item to take action on an opportunity you have, and one to help create opportunities.

It takes discipline to plan the day the night before. If you're overworked and stressed, if you've been running around after your kids all day or on your feet working in a shop, if you've had to deal with difficult customers or sick patients, it's so appealing to get home, pour a glass of something strong and veg out in front of Netflix.

I get it, trust me, and I do it sometimes. You can't seize every day. But if you get into the habit of planning your day the night before, you can avoid traps before they catch you, you can reduce the impact of bad situations, you can get into a strong mindset that helps protect you if something bad happens. You'll sleep better (especially if you add that recurring appointment too) and you'll wake up refreshed and ready to seize the day.

Summary

If you start your day the night before, you'll be prepared to seize the day. In the evening, catch up on messages and emails and reflect on your day, then write yourself a list for the next day. Make it a habit. The more prepared you are before you wake up, the better your chances of seizing the day – every day.

TAKE ACTION

· ·

Write your list for tomorrow.

Follow the three steps in this chapter to include taking action on an opportunity you have and doing something to invite more opportunities into your life.

19
Own the hour (first and last)

Starting my day the night before is part of something I believe has a massive positive impact on my opportunities: I start and end each day in total control. I own the hour at both ends of the day. Let's start in the evening.

End the day well

I've already talked about some of my end-of-day habits, so I'll bring them together here. I think the last hour of the day is massively important, and owning it lets you control how you react to the day you've just had and prepare for the one that's coming. It's an hour you can use to evaluate what has been and what could be, to visualize achieving your goals and letting those visions take root while you sleep. Owning that last hour means you're more likely to rest well, and as any insomniac or parent will tell you, sleep is most definitely not overrated.

The first part of my evening routine is what you just read in the previous chapter. Then, when I get my head on the pillow, I visualize. In Part 1, I shared the visualization routine I do before sleeping – it's something I've done every night for years:

1 I recite a mantra: 'Wealth, success, health, strength, happiness, confidence, non-judgement, abundance, love and gratitude.'
2 I visualize my goals, my vision, my challenges, my problems. I visualize solutions, either in words or in images.

Doing that lets me go to sleep feeling like I'm in control of everything. I have a positive mindset, I'm focused on my goals, and I've given myself a boost by imagining how I'll solve my problems. I'm in control when I go to sleep, and that's how I wake up in the morning.

Start the day well

Imagine you wake up and reach for your phone and you're suddenly overcome with panic – disaster happened overnight, you slept in so you're running late to a meeting that kept you awake because you weren't prepared. You're not feeling great, and the kids are sick, and the dog needs walking, and it's raining, and that panic wells up in you again … You rush around and try to find childcare for the kids, then make a few calls to see if you can join the meeting from home. You put the TV on for the kids and sit with your laptop and a coffee, still in your PJs.

Not a great start to the day, is it? You'd probably be better off staying in bed.

Some of that would be out of your control, but what you can control is your reactions – how you cope, how you behave in the face of adversity. Panic happens when you're not prepared and when you're (unpleasantly) surprised.

Now imagine all those things that were out of your control were still happening, but you owned the hour – you had a set routine for your last hour and first hour of the day. Let's see what that looks like.

You wake up just before your alarm goes off and reach for a glass of water. You sit for a few minutes and breathe slowly and deeply, thinking about nothing but your breath. You notice a few thoughts about the morning's meeting and you let them pass – it's a big meeting but you're well prepared and well rested, so you're feeling confident. You make the bed and notice you're feeling a bit under the weather, so you eat a healthy breakfast and take the dog for a walk to get your blood pumping. The rain is refreshing and it releases the smell of spring from the grass as the sun comes up. You get home, shower, then check your emails – there's been an incident, but you've already got some solutions in your mind. The kids aren't feeling great, but after a fun, playful start to the morning they're up and raring to go in no time. You head off to work feeling energized.

Now doesn't that sound better? There are a few things that made a real difference in this situation:

1 You were well rested. You went to bed on time, having already prepared for the big meeting, so you slept really well and even woke up before your alarm.
2 Instead of checking the outside world, you went inside. Before letting the world's problems in, you strengthened yourself against them by taking time to refresh yourself and spend time quieting your brain.
3 You took care of yourself. With water, breakfast and exercise, you started the day off well.
4 You kept a positive mindset. Rather than instantly looking for the bad in the situation, you focused on the positive – you enjoyed the rain, saw solutions and had fun.

This version of the morning is more likely to lead to a good day – a day you seize and win. The first hour so often dictates the rest of the day, and owning that hour will give you momentum throughout the day. Doing it every day, focusing on consistency, will have a compounding effect and you'll end up maximizing your opportunities.

I'm not the first person to praise good starts, and there are plenty of approaches out there. For example, there's a whole community of people who follow a method called The Miracle Morning, developed by the US success coach Hal Elrod. In his version of the morning, you wake up an hour earlier than usual and do six things, called life SAVERS:

> **Silence** – meditate
> **Affirmations** – say a few positive statements to yourself (think Bruce Willis in *Friends*)
> **Visualization** – imagine your dreams, your goals, the things you want to achieve in life
> **Exercise** – get your heart rate up
> **Reading** – read a book
> **Scribing** – write something, like a journal.

I don't do all this, and I don't think there's any magic-bullet formula for the first or last hour, but it's one way you can own the start of your day.

What works for you?

You've got to figure out what works for you. What gives you energy in the morning? What can you do to make sure you start the day well? This will be different for everyone, but I have five tips that might help you come up with your own plan:

1 Do not make Facebook the first thing you look at.
2 Make your bed.
3 Move your body.
4 Think about opportunities.
5 Get ready to tackle your list.

Let's look at them a bit more closely.

1 Do not make Facebook the first thing you look at

Or Instagram. Or email. Smartphones are seriously clever – they're designed to be addictive. Apps with little red bubbles to tell you something has happened. Noises and vibrations. All those colours. But the trap is that reaching for the phone becomes so natural, second-nature, you let it break down your own confidence and self-esteem before it's had a chance to wake up. We all know that social media is a glossy version of real life. That the dreaded comparison curse will get us into more trouble online than anywhere else. Do you really want to start the day by comparing yourself to someone you met once who is living the dream on some tropical island and raking in millions, being blissfully happy (or so they want you to think)? No. No you don't. Leave your phone alone until you've done a morning routine that leaves you feeling strong, full of energy and confident.

2 Make your bed

If you search for this on YouTube, you'll come up with several videos of a commencement speech Naval Admiral William H. McRaven gave at the University of Texas, Austin in 2014. In that speech, he shares ten lessons he learned in basic Navy Seal training – and one of them is the importance of making your bed every morning. I can't say it better than him, so here's what he said:

'If you make your bed every morning, you will have accomplished the first task of the day. It will give you a small sense of pride, and it will encourage you to do another task, and another, and another. And by the end of the day, that one task completed will have turned into many tasks completed. Making your bed will also reinforce the fact that the little things in life matter; if you can't do the little things right, you'll never be able to do the big things right. And if by chance you have a miserable day, you will come home to a bed that is made. That you made. And a made bed gives you encouragement that tomorrow will be better. So if you want to change the world, start off by making your bed.'

3 Move your body

You don't have to run ten kilometres or do a full-on workout or a Bikram Yoga session, but just moving your body in a controlled way will help you really embody your mental strength and energize you. I have a gym at home so I can use that in the morning if I want to, or go for a walk or even just do a bit of stretching. I don't do the same thing every day, but I make sure I don't just go from bed to chair to car to chair.

4 Think about opportunities

When your mind is fresh and you're full of energy, you're more likely to make neural connections and think of solutions to problems and have ideas – it's the ideal time to nurture opportunities. Consciously think about opportunities – the ones you want or have, ones you might be able to create or take. Let yourself get excited.

5 Get ready to tackle your list

You'll have your list from the night before; it's good to get your mind into the right space to tackle the thing in the number-one spot. It should be the biggest, most important, juiciest thing. To use Brian Tracy's analogy, get ready to eat that juicy frog. You might want to visualize completing the task, or think about how you'll approach it, or even set your mind to the reward you'll give yourself when it's done. Get obsessed about ticking that first item off (and forget obsessing over the rest of the list).

Starting the day off with an hour that you control, that you design to put you in the best possible place, mentally and physically, to tackle the day is the best way to maximize your opportunities. Control beats overwhelm, and starting off with everything under control will help you keep that approach for the whole day.

Summary

Owning the first and last hour of the day will let you focus on the control you have over your day, giving you the attitude and power to seize it. Ending the day by reflecting and planning, as I recommended in the previous chapter, then visualizing your goals and how you might solve problems will set you up for a restful, rejuvenating night. Starting the day by looking after your own mind and body, by feeling in control and by getting excited about opportunities, will set you up for a positive day that you can win.

TAKE ACTION
. . . .

Come up with a routine for the first and last hour of your day.

Think about:

- planning the next day
- visualizing your goals
- sleeping well
- preparing your mind and body
- inviting opportunity
- eating the frog.

20
Routine = Results

What does your ideal day look like? Do you even know? I think you can design it, and that's what this chapter is about.

It's no secret that I'm a big fan of compartmentalizing my diary. I've got recurring appointments for everything from staff meetings to romantic dinners, gym visits to golf with my son. It's not the easiest thing to stick with at first, but if you follow the process and follow your own rules, I guarantee you you'll notice opportunities having a much bigger impact on your life (or your money back! Only kidding.).

I'm such a mega fan that I devoted a hefty appendix in my book *Start Now, Get Perfect Later* to the subject, also called 'Routine = Results'. (It's brilliant, you should read it.) The idea behind the phrase is that you can manage your routines to drive your results – planning and controlling each day will help you create opportunities and use them, one after the other, to help you win at life.

I bet something that's come up for you while you've been reading this book is that you just don't have the time to do XYZ. You're already so busy, you don't have time to read or get out and meet people or research an opportunity that's on the table.

I call bullshit on that. We all have 1,441 minutes in a day. You have the same number of minutes in each of your days as Oprah Winfrey and Bill Gates.

You can't *manage* time, it's inevitable. It will tick along at exactly the same pace, day in, day out. It's not stopping for you. All you can do is manage your life in the time you have. Manage your energy and emotions, your priorities and productivity.

Managing your life starts with managing your diary. I go into all this in detail in that appendix, but I want to touch on some of the points here and give you a taster of the processes that can really help boost opportunity, every day in your life.

Compartmentalizing your diary

I'm going to be honest, when I started all this managing my day stuff, I was so bored. I was a cool artist, remember, and I thought I was killing my spontaneity and my mojo and my vibe if I built what I thought of as walls in my life. Wasn't I just doing what I'd been fighting against authority over my whole life – wasn't I limiting my freedom?

Well, as you know by now, that young artist had a lot to learn. Sometimes I wish I could go back and give him a good talking to, but I know he would never have listened to some rich bloke in a bright-red sports car.

What I know now is that it's that tightly managed diary that gives me freedom. It's the compartmentalization of my day that lets me create and take opportunities all the time. It's not boring at all – it lets me squeeze every last drop out of every single day.

It's a simple concept really: block time in your diary for everything you want and need to do, starting with the important stuff and working your way down the importance scale. But I don't want you to do that quite yet; first I want you to analyse how you spend your days right now, for 21 days.

I've put a template for this online, you can get it at robmoore.com/opportunity-resources, or you can make your own. It's simple:

1 Set out your day in 30-minute timeslots (or 15-minute slots if your day is more granular).
2 Fill in each slot with: W for work; R for rest; S for social, family and so on; O for opportunity.
3 Specify what you did in a few words (under O, note whether you worked on preparing for them or dealing with one you already have).

4 Be completely honest – you're only lying to yourself if you're not.

Do this for 21 days, then come back.

Hey, how are you? It's been a while. OK, you have your work log. Now you can look at it and start making plans. Where did you waste time? Is there a pattern? You might be able to spot times when you were low on energy – that's a good time for a coffee or a walk. Maybe at some points you were in flow – that's great, make a note to block out time for concentrated, deep work. What about distraction? Plan to avoid it or do a different kind of task at those times. Look at all the things you did – can you batch your tasks? It takes about 25 minutes to refocus after switching tasks, so this could save you masses of time.

Now you're ready to compartmentalize your diary.

KLAs, KRAs, IGTs

In *Life Leverage* I introduced a whole load of TLAs (three-letter abbreviations!) and three of them form the basis of creating your ideal day:

> **KLA – Key Life Area.** The most important things in your life. Your rocks.
> **KRA – Key Result Area.** The things that will move you forward in your life. Your pebbles.
> **IGT – Income-Generating Task.** The things that will make you money. Your sand.

Imagine you're sitting at a table and in front of you is a big glass jar, a pile of rocks, a pile of pebbles and a pile of sand. You have to fit everything in the jar. If you start with the sand, you might fit in a few pebbles, but the rocks will have no chance. Instead, you need to start with the rocks, then the pebbles will fit around them, then the sand will fit in the gaps.

That's a pretty well-known analogy for prioritizing, and it works. Only we never do it. Why? It's so easy to get caught up in the tide of daily demands. But if you want to seize opportunities, you have to master the art of prioritization.

It starts in the diary, and it starts with blocking out time for these three things. Literally block out time so you absolutely can't do anything else. Start with the rocks – KLAs – and make sure they reflect your values and the things that are most important in your life. Your weekly date night. Your Saturday morning standing on the soggy side-line watching your daughter play football. Your gym sessions. Your Friday movie day with the whole family. Your saxophone practice. Your book club.

Then add the pebbles – your KRAs. You'll probably have between three and seven of these, and they will depend on what sort of work or other activities you're focused on. For a freelance marketer, they might be blogging, social media content and writing eBooks. For someone in property, maybe managing listings, talking to investors, viewing properties, coordinating solicitors and agents. Only you can know what your KRAs are – focus on the few things that bring 80 per cent of your results.

Last, pour in the sand: add your tasks to the mix. What little things do you need to do on a daily basis to keep the money rolling in?

Your jar is now full. Look at the table again – next to your big jar, you'll see two smaller jars, one about half the size of the other. This is where you can have some fun.

70–20–10

I get bored easily. I'm always looking for the next exciting thing to work on, and I prefer to say 'yes' (or some 'yes' version of 'no', like 'yes, but not now'). I'm an opportunity junkie. So I have to make sure my strategy and my diary let that happen.

As an entrepreneur, I manage this by taking the 70–20–10 approach: I spend 70 per cent of my time on the main thing,

20 per cent on the thing I'm growing and 10 per cent on the wild card.

Let's break that down. The 70 per cent is my main business, my bread and butter, the thing that brings in the cash. I make sure 70 per cent of my week is spent on that, and I do it when I compartmentalize my diary. I can see it laid out in front of me – I can make sure I actually spend 70 per cent of my time on that.

The 20 per cent is on a different business or project, perhaps something that's new or growing, or something that's not bringing in as much money – yet. Again, I set aside 20 per cent of my time for that.

Then there's the 10 per cent – the crazy new thing, the wild card, the passion project. It might be risky, it might be uncertain, it might be totally left field. This is what always gets squeezed out if you don't have those diary barriers up, but it's so important to include it. If you're struggling to be excited by the 70 per cent (because let's face it, that happens sometimes), then this 10 per cent will keep your spark going.

Companies like Google do this really well – they carve out time for their employees to work on their own projects, which don't have to be in line with their strategy or the employee's objectives at all. It makes for more engaged, happier people. Be like Google: give yourself the fun 10 per cent.

Design your diary

I might be an expert diary designer now, but I wasn't always this way. I had to sit down with my assistant and go through a process to reset my diary and rebuild it – and it was so effective, that's what we do every year. Here's the process:

1 Scrap it and redo it – when life is quiet (August and December are usually good for this), clear out your diary – delete appointments you don't need, scale it all back and check with

life and business partners to make sure you've got the right KLAs and KRAs in there. Think about your priorities and opportunities, what you want to do more or less of, and adjust.

2 Share your diary with important people in your life – make sure anyone who puts appointments in your diary has access to it. It's obvious, but believe me, you'll be in a mess very quickly if you don't. Put your diary in the cloud – Google, iCal, something everyone can use – and make it visible to those you want to see it.

3 Sync your diary across all your devices – again, obvious, but this will save you a whole lot of trouble.

4 Block out the most important time first, one year ahead – holidays, school events, date nights, health and fitness, strategy for your business, exams, big opportunities – your KLAs and KRAs.

5 Block out the most important time in your most productive time – keep your work log close by when you're blocking time, and listen to yourself. Put the important work at the times you work best – don't let someone fill up your flow time with unproductive coffee meetings.

6 Use the recurring and invitee features. Digital calendars are clever – spend a bit of time figuring out all the tricks (or, better yet, get your VA to do it). One small thing here: make sure you choose colours you like to look at. You don't have to stare at a brown screen if you don't want to.

7 Put enough detail and agendas in the 'notes' section – the last thing you need is a vague appointment you have no idea about. You might have written 'wedding' only to realize it wasn't just a case of putting on a suit, you had to give a speech, too (or, even worse, say vows).

8 Update/redo your diary every six months or year – don't get complacent, keep it fresh so it keeps working for you.

9 Create alternative diary systems for school holidays and holidays – you won't be 'on it' all the time; when you're

on a family holiday, that flow time might be the best time to play with the kids.

When you've got your diary full, sit back and bask in its glory, then get on with your life. Get a blank copy of the work log and do it again for 21 days. This will give you a comparison, then you can make adjustments until your compartmentalized diary fits you perfectly.

Don't fall into the trap of thinking that routines are boring. Having a routine will literally change your life – you'll get more out of your time, and you'll have the freedom and flexibility to see and take opportunities.

Summary

You can manage your routines to drive your results. We all have the same number of hours in a day, and we can't manage time – it will pass whatever we do. We can manage our own diaries. By planning and controlling each day, you will be able to create opportunities and use them. Start by prioritizing – what's most important in your life? Then track your life for 21 days – what's working and what isn't? Then compartmentalize your diary and monitor the results so you can adjust it until it works for you.

TAKE ACTION

. . . .

Sort your diary out.

Go through this chapter again and follow the processes.

1 Figure out your KLAs, KRAs and IGTs.
2 Do a 21-day work log.
3 Compartmentalize your diary.
4 Monitor your new schedule for 21 days and adjust until it works.

21

Selfish and selfless

Guilt sucks. It's one of those things that every entrepreneur – probably every human – knows all too well. It's often labelled as a useless, destructive emotion – it's energy draining and pointless because it so often manifests in beating yourself up about something you've done (or not done) and can no longer fix.

It's something you'll need to learn to deal with on your journey to taking more opportunities.

I feel it too. A while ago, I wrote a poem about guilt, and I'd like to share it with you here.

Every day; the guilt

Every day guilt consumes me

When I'm working, guilt I'm not with my family

When I'm with my family, guilt I'm not working

So many ideas and guilt that I'm not implementing them all

When I make money, the guilt that others don't have any

When I start tasks, guilt that I don't finish them

When I hurt people, the guilt of how I made them feel

When I fail, the guilt of the people I have let down

I don't know if the guilt ever goes away

Sometimes it eats me up inside

In a sadistic way I think it drives us to spend our time wisely, do the best we can, and try to be kind to others

I think it is part of being human

Do you feel it too?

There you go. Bet you never knew I was a poet!

The importance of guilt

I dislike feeling guilty as much as the next person, but I disagree that it's useless. In fact, I think it's a really important emotion we should pay attention to. I think it's the feedback that tells us if we're out of balance on the selfish–selfless scale.

Everything is a paradox and everything needs balance. I would struggle to think of a situation where being at the extreme end of a scale is beneficial to you and the people around you. So I think we all need to be a bit selfless and a bit selfish.

If you're too selfish, people will challenge you, they'll dislike you, they'll judge you in a negative way. You'll be outcast and, at the extreme, maybe even imprisoned or killed. But you'll also be hurting yourself – you'll miss out on the genuine joy and sense of fulfilment that comes with helping and serving others. Importantly, you'll be closing the door to opportunity because you won't be able to see beyond your own reflection.

If you're too selfless, you risk becoming weak and downtrodden, exhausted and irrelevant. You'll be the proverbial lemming walking off the cliff; no one likes a martyr and, by being selfless all the time, you'll end up making other people feel guilty. You'll also miss out on the opportunities you might get if you focus on yourself a bit – your personal development, your own life.

So if you want to maximize your opportunities, I think you need to keep your selfish and selfless sides in balance.

Managing guilt

Guilt will always be there. It's inevitable. You can't expect to follow your own path and not feel guilty some of the time – you can't please all of the people all of the time, as they say. You'll feel guilty towards yourself (which might come out as resentment) when you give more than you receive, and guilt in the form of regret when you receive more than you give.

If you can rethink guilt, and see it as a compass, then you can start to manage it. I think there are seven ways to manage guilt.

1 *Accept it.* Guilt is bad, but suppressed guilt is worse — what you suppress you will be forced to express. Instead of trying to ignore it or bury it or hide it, just accept it, distance yourself from it and see it as a feedback emotion. Use it.

2 *Understand it.* Remember that guilt is a feedback emotion, it will help you balance being selfish and selfless. It can tell you if you're focusing on the wrong tasks, the wrong areas of your life, the wrong people. Pay attention and adjust.

3 *Plan and compartmentalize your KLAs and KRAs.* Follow the approach in Chapter 20 to make sure you're making room for what's important.

4 *Keep tabs on it.* Notice when guilt starts to take over and eat away at you, then stop, step back, be kind to yourself and figure out what it's trying to tell you.

5 *Love and accept yourself.* Guilt is compounding — the more you let it in, the more it will win. It's always a good idea to treat yourself the way you would your best friend … When you're being hard on yourself, ask the question: 'Would I say that to my best friend?'

6 *Let go of what you can't control.* You'll kill yourself trying to control the uncontrollable; instead, focus on how you react to those things — that's all you can do.

7 *Don't try to be all things to all people.* A sure-fire way to be great at nothing is to try to be great at everything. Yes, set goals; yes, try to be a better person. But you can't be everything. Know yourself and be yourself — the best version you can be.

Protect your time

That last point is a really big one when it comes to guilt. You really can't be everything. You can't always be the one who jumps in to help, the one who saves the day, the one who solves the problem.

There's a brilliant Polish proverb that translates as 'Not my circus, not my monkeys.' It basically means leave me out of your problems, they're not mine to solve. If you're a natural problem solver, you'll feel compelled to help other people, offer advice, fix things, but that is rarely constructive – you'll end up burning out and pissing off a lot of people who didn't ask for help. When you get the urge to be everything to everyone, think MONKEY and step away.

Sometimes that's not easy, especially if you're in demand. Some days I feel like I'm surrounded by people clawing at me trying to take a piece of me – it's stressful and not very pleasant, to say the least. Some of them will play at your guilt to get you to do what they want. Notice that when it happens and refuse to be manipulated.

Your time is precious – it's your life. Give too much of it away and you won't have any left for your life right now, let alone to embrace new opportunities.

For me, the two best ways to protect my time from other people are to have a rock-solid diary (see the previous chapter to make yours) and to learn to say 'no'.

Prioritize what's important

Guilt will usually rear its head when you're not focusing enough on the important stuff – your KLAs. When you're missing your family (or they're missing you), when you're neglecting a hobby, when you're missing payments.

There's really only one way to prevent this from happening and that's to fix the important things in your life, to make them unmovable appointments in your diary.

The more you do this, the better you'll be at sticking to your own agenda. If you have the important things in mind when you plan your diary, you're automatically scheduling less guilt.

And by doing all of this, you'll also avoid the guilt of missing an opportunity – the guilt you feel towards yourself if you miss your shot, if your one chance sails by.

Summary

You need to find a balance between being selfish and selfless. Everyone needs to be a bit of both; fall too far towards one extreme and you'll experience guilt, which isn't anyone's idea of fun. There are ways to deal with guilt, including accepting and understanding it, and making sure you're not trying to be everything to everyone. Protect what's important in your life and give yourself the time to embrace opportunities.

TAKE ACTION

How guilty are you feeling?

On a scale of 1 to 10, where's your guilt right now? What is that telling you? Think about what it might be signalling:

- not enough focus on KLAs?
- missing opportunities?
- resentment due to not enough self-care?

Write down up to three things you can do to bring your selfish–selfless scale back into balance.

22

LMD – leverage, manage, do

If you have a 'to do' list, ditch it and pay attention: there's a better way.

We've come back to scheduling and planning a few times throughout this book, and we've looked at how to manage your schedule. Now we'll look at managing tasks. This will help you free up time for opportunity hunting.

I don't have 'to do' lists any more. They're the best possible way to get overwhelmed and become unproductive. If you want to move your life forward, seizing every day, taking opportunities and winning more than you lose, then you need to stop spending time on things that are not important for you. If those things need to be done, you can get other people to do them.

Instead of a 'to do' list, you need a 'to leverage' list.

Let's start with a list of the tasks that need to be done. Remember this is the list you'll make every night to prepare for the next day, so don't make it an epic list of all the things you need to get done in the next five years. Here are a few pointers:

1 Include a maximum of seven things.
2 Put them in order of importance: KLA, KRA, IGT, the rest …
3 Always start with the first thing and *do not move on until it's done.*

Now you've done that, we're going to break the list into three columns. I call this the L1, M2, DL system: Leverage first, Manage second, Do last.

So you need three columns, labelled (left to right) Leverage, Manage, Do.

Look at your list. What on that list could someone else do? You might be brilliant at mopping the floor, but could a cleaner do it instead? What about that invoice you need to send, could a VA do it? Or the property you need to view, could a partner take your place? Whatever you can leverage — give to someone else — put into the Leverage column.

OK, you still have three tasks and two columns. The Manage column is for the things you will need to chase — you'll have to follow up on the tasks in the Leverage column to make sure they get done, after all. Finally, the Do column is for the things *only you* can do.

Compare your two lists — doesn't your 'to leverage' list look so much better than your original 'to do' list? If you've identified three tasks of the six on your list that you can leverage, you've doubled your results in half the time. Bingo! More time for opportunity nurturing.

Summary

It's time to level up your 'to do' list — make a 'to leverage' list instead! Write down a list of your tasks, in order of importance, then separate out the ones you can leverage out to other people. In a three-column list, put the Leverage tasks (left), the Manage tasks (leveraged things to monitor) and the Do tasks (things only you can do). Hey presto — more efficiency, less overwhelm and plenty of time for opportunities!

TAKE ACTION

Create your own 'to leverage' list and attack item number 1.

23
(Re)start every day fresh

The best thing about winning at life by seizing the day is that every day you get to start again. The sun will always go down on one day and come up on another (unless you live in the Arctic or Antarctica).

Who says you need to bring the baggage of yesterday into today?

Let yesterday go. It's happened, it's gone, let it go. ('Can't hold it back anymore …' – I swear they wrote that song to be an earworm.) I don't mean be blind to the past – it's really important to reflect on what's happened and learn from it, so you're more likely to win the day tomorrow. What I mean is you should live in the present – don't get stuck in yesterday's mistakes or missed opportunities.

Guilt and regret are two signs that you're holding onto yesterday too tightly. You can feel it in the pit of your stomach – the churning that you can't control, the surge of hormones that makes your fingers tingle and your head spin. Listen to that automatic, biological response and pinpoint the cause. What are you dragging along from yesterday? Why can't you let it go? What could you do to leave it behind?

Memento mori

Back to our old pal Seneca. The Stoics had a wonderful way of staying in the present and seizing the day. *Memento mori*: a reminder that death is inevitable. They would have ways of reminding themselves that they were going to die in order to remind themselves to live. The Stoic philosopher Epictetus taught his students that when they kissed their loved ones, they should remember they are mortal. (Heavy, right? That makes the bedtime story routine a bit harder.)

A lot of people would tell you not to be morbid. To look on the bright side. To stop thinking about death.

I disagree – I'm with the Stoics on this one. Death is the only thing we're guaranteed in life.

Sit with that uncomfortable fact for a moment.

Now think about something that's bothering you from yesterday or the day before that. Now remember you're going to die. Does that thing seem a bit less important?

Keep the ultimate end in mind and it will be easier to let go, easier to focus on what's important, easier to seize every day as if it's your last. The time is always NOW – not later. Not tomorrow. And definitely not yesterday.

The more you focus on the now and learning from the things that didn't sit right about yesterday rather than letting them drown you, the more you'll grab every opportunity, the more good days you'll have. Win the day, day after day after day, and you'll win at life. Of course you'll lose some, but letting those losses go and pushing for a win tomorrow is all you can do.

New day, new you?

When was the last time you said, 'I'll start tomorrow', or 'I'll start Monday', or 'I'll start next month'? The new diet. The new training regime. The new business. The novel.

It's so easy to put things off until the next 'good' time to start.

Monday's good, but the start of next month would be better, wouldn't it? Or hang on, even better if the start of the month was a Monday. Oh wait, January 1st would probably be better. Oh, and if January 1st was a Monday … now that's worth waiting for!

Always putting off being the 'new you'.

But you and I both know the reality: it's all arbitrary. Dates are meaningless. Humans have walked the earth for tens of thousands of years, but we've only had this calendar since October 1582. The human in you doesn't give a shit if it's Monday; if the sun comes up, it's a good day to be you.

This concept of 'new you' is really misleading. You've convinced yourself you're not good enough, not happy enough, not smart enough, not good-looking enough, not fit enough, not wealthy enough, not successful enough, and you've decided that you'll start being more of that thing tomorrow. Or Monday. Or next month. Or January …

It will never happen. You know why? Because until you accept that you are who you are, you'll never stick to the new thing. It doesn't fit with you. You don't recognize yourself in it. It doesn't feel natural.

I absolutely believe that we can all improve in every area of our lives. But when you don't really know, accept and love yourself, you won't commit to real change because you won't be where you need to be in order to start.

Chapter 6 in Part 2 was about getting to know yourself. Really learning who you are. I bet there are gaps all over the place between who you are and who you *think* you are, and they're probably not favourable. You're probably judging yourself really harshly, beating yourself up, being unfair to yourself and, as a result, you're setting unrealistic goals for the 'new you'. And that's why you never start.

Think about an area where you're being hard on yourself and continually putting off the new start. What are you missing? What are you really like? What's in the mirror that you're not seeing? What is holding you back from change?

When you start to delve deep into yourself (brace yourself, because it's a crazy journey), you go through a process of discovery, shock and acceptance. The shock is that you are *you*. You're not discovering someone new, you're exactly who you are. But delving deep within will reveal you to yourself so clearly that you'll understand *why* you are who you are. And you'll understand *how* to change.

Then, when the sun comes up, you'll start.

Summary

Death is the only thing we're guaranteed in life, so why live in the past? Seize every day and don't let yesterday drag you down. Reflect, learn and move on. Life only happens NOW – not tomorrow and not yesterday. If you want to make change, start now; be you, every time the sun comes up.

TAKE ACTION

What baggage are you carrying around from yesterday? Think of something that you haven't let go. What can you do to leave it behind? *Memento mori* – remember your mortality. Is it really that important? If it is, what can you do to learn from it or correct it tomorrow? Make sure that's on your list before you go to bed.

PART 5

How to 'win at life'

24
What is success?

Success (noun): the accomplishment of an aim or purpose.

What is success to you?

Is it having loads of money? Or having loads of free time? Is it mastering a musical instrument or a sport, a trade or a skill? Is it seeing your name in lights or on the bookshelves? Is it having a qualification or a family?

If you look at the definition above, the clue is right there: success is the accomplishment of an aim or purpose, so success depends on your goals.

If your goal is to have $1 million, then you will consider yourself successful when you have $1 million. If your goal is to master a martial art, then you will consider yourself successful when you have a black belt in karate. If your goal is to raise your family in your dream house, then you'll consider yourself successful when you're tucking the kids in bed in your castle.

Simple, right?

Where opportunity meets success

Nope. Because this isn't true. Because if your goal is to have $1 million, then by the time you have $1 million, your goal has shifted upwards to $5 million, so you can't consider yourself successful.

This is what I live for. This is growth and progress and challenge. This is striving for something more, something better, every time the sun rises.

This is also where opportunity meets success – it's the triad that keeps you moving forward. You have a goal, and opportunity helps you meet that and be successful, and in the process your goal shifts, bringing in another opportunity and so on, for ever and ever, until you have billions in the bank.

Goal by goal, aim by aim, purpose by purpose, you can chase success this way. You can measure it, track your progress, keep pushing your goals forward and upward.

But there's a different dimension to success, too, and it overrides all the rest if it isn't there. Legendary author Maya Angelou said it perfectly: 'Success is liking yourself, liking what you do, and liking how you do it.'

You can have $1 million in the bank, but if you don't like what you do, are you successful? You can wear that black belt, but if you don't like yourself, are you successful? You can live in that dream house, but if you don't like what you do to pay the mortgage, are you successful?

In Part 4 we spent a lot of time looking at systems and processes you can put in place to seize the day, to get more wins than losses. That's all based on prioritization, and your top priorities – the foundations of your life and the things that determine your success, however you define it – always come first. That's a good way to set yourself up for success.

If you've got your most important things – your KLAs – prioritized, then you're on track to liking what you do and how you do it; liking yourself comes in Part 2 – getting to know yourself. For me, that's been through mentorship, coaching, personal development and therapy. You might have a different way of doing it (or you might already know all about yourself … impressive!).

Beware

Liking yourself can feel weird if you've programmed yourself to be self-loathing, self-deprecating and self-flagellating. And a very easy way to pull yourself away from success is through the comparison curse – comparing yourself and your life to the shiny, glitzy, pol-ished, filtered, social-media versions of other people's lives. That's something to watch out for and avoid at all costs because, at best, it will make you suspicious and, at worst, it will make you spiral into self-hatred.

It's not just the comparison curse that jeopardizes your success, or your journey to it. It's also extremes. Throughout this book I've talked about paradox and balance – everything has an opposite, everything needs a counterweight. As much as you might be com-pelled to push at all costs, it's good to pull yourself back a bit, too.

When you have a goal that fires you up, that you want to achieve more than anything else, and an opportunity that helps you progress towards that goal, it's easy to get tunnel vision. I've been there. A lot. But you risk going to the extreme and staying there for too long – being too greedy, being too selfish – and under that kind of tension things tend to snap: your motivation, your capacity to work, your relationship. You focus too hard on one goal and forget the rest.

Swing too far the other way, and you lose momentum, you stop working and you close off to opportunities. You have no chance of meeting your goal, and you stop liking what you do and how you do it.

It's balance that predicts true success. The ability to push for that financial goal while you strive to nurture your family. To push for that sporting goal while you aim for promotion.

Keep track

When you're seeking balance, there will be days when you push more and days when you need a push. For those days, when it can be easy to forget what the point was in the first place, it's good to be able to see how you're doing.

Back in Chapter 3, on visualization, I mentioned SMART goals – goals that are Specific, Measurable, Achievable, Realistic and Time-bound. They're a favourite of companies around the world (we use this basic set-up at Progressive) so you might be thinking 'YAWN' but, trust me, they work. And you can use this framework for any goal you have.

The reason I'm mentioning it here is because, if you have a SMART goal, you've automatically got a measurement element in there, so you can track your progress. Here's a brief breakdown:

> **Specific** – make your goal as tight as possible – think 'Buy house 15 East Street' rather than 'Be happy with my home'.
> **Measurable** – you have to be able to measure the outcome and, ideally, your progress to the outcome.
> **Attainable** – if you set yourself the goal of swimming in an underground lake on Mars, you're only setting yourself up for failure.
> **Relevant** – make it something you care about; it should align with your values and what's important in your life.
> **Time-bound** – give yourself a deadline, unless you're happy for it to stretch out for all eternity, because it will.

I want to focus on the M – Measurable. Whenever you set a goal, before you start working towards it, ask yourself, 'What does success look like?' Of course, your goal will probably shift as you move towards it, but you need a horizon when you start out, otherwise you'll be steering the ship on a strange course. Think to yourself:

- What is success?
- How will I know if I've succeeded?
- What are the steps I need to take to reach the goal?
- How can I measure those steps?

When you're clear on those things, your goal will come into sharper focus. And when a goal is in sharper focus, you're more likely to achieve it.

Summary

Success is different for everyone, and it's directly related to your goals, aims and purpose. When you've achieved what you set out to do, you will feel successful. Except that doesn't happen; your goal shifts the closer you get to it, and you're on a constant journey. Beware the comparison curse and of extremes — they will derail you. Instead, keep your eye on the prize — set out a SMART goal and make sure you measure your progress so you know when you've succeeded.

TAKE ACTION
. . . .
What does success mean to you?

Write down three elements of success for you, right now, in your life. Are these different to what they would have been five years ago? Notice if the goals would be the same only bigger.

Choose one of your goals and turn it into a SMART goal.

How will you measure success?

25
The happiness of progress

I want you to think back to a time when you felt really low. Perhaps you were depressed. You had no motivation, you weren't enjoying life, you couldn't see the upside in anything. How did it feel? Did you feel like you were in a rut? Like you were stuck, stagnant, not moving?

Sometimes to understand something, you have to look at the exact opposite.

To understand happiness, look at unhappiness. Unhappiness is stagnation, therefore …

Happiness is growth. Happiness is progress. Happiness is moving towards something, working hard to overcome a challenge or solve a problem. *Happiness is progress towards a worthy goal.*

Growing pains and ecstasies

OK, now think about the last time you were happy. I mean *elated*. What were you doing? Why did you feel so good? I think it's safe to say we reach the peak of our elation when we've achieved some-thing difficult. Something that's worth celebrating. Something meaningful. Like solving a big problem in your life – or someone else's. Like climbing a mountain – literally or metaphorically.

I really believe that happiness is a choice, to a large extent. You can *choose* to be grateful for your challenges, you can *choose* to be happy in the moment, you can *choose* to see the upside. But if you're consciously avoiding big challenges because you want things to be easier rather than for you to be better, if you avoid pain at all costs and want a simple life, you'll miss out on the deeper sense of satisfaction that's the other side of the problem. You don't get a deep sense of confidence in who you are when you meditate a joyful feeling.

Happiness isn't just a feeling of contentment; it's achieving something, growing, overcoming, trying and succeeding.

Of course, we're animals, so it comes down to biology – there are a collection of chemicals in the brain, including oxytocin, endorphins and dopamine, that make it extra brilliant when we overcome a hardship, when we win. Winning is good. It's like setting off a confetti cannon of hormones in our heads. Yay!

I believe that feeling – that real happiness – happens when you're constantly striving for something and you succeed – it's the meaningful win, the goal that matters.

Yet when you're heading towards your goal with tunnel vision, when you focus too much on the outcome, at the light at the end of that tunnel, you miss the *journey* to that goal. You reach the destination and realize it's been moved. That can be a never-ending pursuit, but that's the point. If happiness was a goal and I achieved it, what am I going to do next?

It's not just about the goal. It's not just about the journey. It's about both. It's a balance. To be truly happy, you need successes you can celebrate, but you can't hang up your coat for the last time and spend your retirement watching the cat lick its arse. (You're welcome for that juicy picture.) There's a quote from Dr David J. Lieberman that I like: 'You're either growing or dying; living or decaying.'

Dr Lieberman has studied happiness, and one of the conclusions he has drawn is that you need discomfort and challenge in order to give you the meaning and the goal. Speaking at the Project Inspire Convention 2016, he said: 'If you only seek comfort, you'll end up short circuiting your ability to gain self-esteem.' You can't have the win without the struggle and challenge.

Get into flow

A really strong indicator of whether you're progressing towards a worthy goal is the 'flow' state. You've probably experienced this – it's when you're in the zone, when you're really stuck into something and you lose all sense of time and the outside world; it's just you and that task. It often happens when you're concentrating really hard on a big juicy problem – you're completely consumed by it and invested in it. It takes every ounce of brain power and energy you have. It's deliciously difficult.

I think noticing flow and trying to make it happen more often is a great way to stay on track with a worthy goal towards happiness. Here's how you could do that:

When you're doing the 21-day work log from Chapter 20 in Part 4, make a special note of times when you felt in flow. At the time, or at the end of the day (don't leave it too long or you might forget), write down the conditions around that experience:

- What were you doing?
- Where were you?
- What tools or equipment were you using?
- What was around in your environment? Were you distracted?
- How did you feel? Hot? Cold? Energized? Nervous?

The more you remember, the better you'll be able to analyse the information after 21 days.

When you have completed the log, look through specifically at your 'flow' moments:

- What do they all have in common?
- How could you replicate that on a regular basis?

Then all you have to do is set yourself up for flow. Schedule it in, prepare the things you need, switch off devices if that helps. Get yourself a worthy goal. Invite flow.

This might happen at the juncture between your passion and profession. Or any two areas of your life. Noticing that could open up new opportunities for you to explore that more deeply.

Find a worthy goal

If you want to grow, you have to strive; meditating in front of Netflix ain't gonna get you there. You need to win, compete, evolve and solve, and thrive to be alive.

One way to make sure you're working towards a worthy goal – one that will give you a huge happiness pay-out if you achieve it – is to pick the biggest problem in your life, roll up your sleeves and get stuck in. Solve it. Get. It. Done.

Got an idea for a worthy goal? Turn it into a SMART goal (remember: Specific, Measurable, Attainable, Relevant and Time-bound) and figure out when you'll be able to get into flow while you're solving it.

Doing this means you're literally engineering success and happiness – in its redefined sense.

Now, I suggest doing this with every problem and challenge in your life. You need to solve them anyway, so why not make them all part of the journey and the destination? You're opening new opportunities with every challenge you tackle: if you struggle against it, you might reach flow; and if you succeed and you move the problem, you've solved one of your problems. Win-win!

Summary

Happiness isn't lying idle in a hammock, swinging above white sand and listening to the calming waves crash under a blue sky. Really, it isn't. True happiness comes when you're working towards a meaningful goal. Try to engineer the flow state – the zone you get into when you can really stick your teeth into a problem. Then you'll be happy – and you'll have one less problem to deal with.

TAKE ACTION
· ·
Choose a worthy goal. What challenging problem are you facing? It could be business-related, money-related or relationship-related, for example.

1 Turn the problem into a goal.
2 Write out the SMART attributes of the goal. Be clear about measurement.
3 Assuming you've tracked your flow, set yourself up to get into a flow state as much as possible while you're working on the problem.
4 Track your progress – and remember to enjoy the feeling of happiness it brings!

26

Commit and get accountable

Now it's really time to knuckle down. This is the chapter where we make sure you take your opportunities and get shit done. No excuses.

Start now, get perfect later

The best way to get shit done is to *JFDI – just f***ing do it*. People really struggle with that; I blame our inner perfectionist. But the fact is that you'll never be perfect. It will never be exactly how you want it. You'll never be totally finished or completely ready. If you wait for that moment, you'll die waiting. If you push for that moment, you'll push yourself over the edge.

Perfectionism feeds into procrastination. They're in the ultimate unhealthy relationship. Perfectionism gives procrastination its *raison d'être*. Add to that great pair the fact that we're already overwhelmed and we are excellent at lying to ourselves, and *voilà*! The best way to achieve absolutely nothing.

The way I overcome all this is by doing stuff. I just start, and I improve and tweak and adjust as I go along. US real-estate guru Grant Cardone talks about this, too. I've interviewed Grant a couple of times for my podcast and, in one interview, he was talking about writing books. He says for him, it's better to publish a book with typos than to publish no book. The theory is that he gets it out there, people point out the mistakes, and they can be corrected in the second edition. I think it's a great idea (obviously I don't need to do that, because this book is perfect;)).

I knew a lot of people (almost everyone, if they're honest) struggle with the same issues around this, so I wrote a book called *Start Now. Get Perfect Later.* It's filled with short, practical chapters taking you through the reasons for not getting things in action, then the ways to make it happen. I'm going to outline a few here.

- *Procrastination:* we all do it, but don't label yourself. Recognize that it has a function and get on with it.
- *Get help:* if you need help, ask for it.
- *Perfectionism:* it won't serve you and it's unachievable.
- *Do it now:* don't put off until tomorrow what you can start today. The only time is NOW.
- *Beware multitasking:* task jumping is a terrible idea – it will kill your productivity. Try flow instead.
- *No worries:* that worst-case scenario almost never happens, so don't sweat it.
- *Be decisive:* make a decision already. The wrong decision is usually better than no decision.
- *Push yourself:* go slightly beyond your capacity to keep things exciting, but avoid decision fatigue.
- *Set goals:* make them clear and visualize them.
- *Prioritize:* only work on tasks that are for you; leverage the rest.
- *Accountability:* get some!
- *FOMO (fear of missing out):* notice it but don't get sucked in.
- *Imagine the worst:* think ahead, then accept the risk.
- *GOYA (get off your arse) and JFDI!*
- *It's not final:* change your mind if you need to.

If you want more detail on these points, you can read the book. At the heart of it is this: you just have to get moving. Do something. Take the first logical step. Then take the next one. Break through your fear, perfectionism and procrastination and *start*.

Because an opportunity will soon shrivel and die if you don't keep it moving.

Get some accountability

Who's the easiest person to lie to? You, of course. You lie to yourself all the time and don't notice it, and it's the number-one reason you don't reach your goals. Denial is a way of lying to yourself. Refusing to accept that something isn't going well, ignoring the elephant in the room, not seeing things for how they really are.

The best way to overcome that, to stop you from lying to yourself, is to get some external accountability – get some people around you who will tell you the truth and hold you to your goals.

This is a really big part of what I do. As a mentor, I guide people through being an entrepreneur and, while I'm lovely and cuddly and supportive most of the time (really I am), sometimes I hit them with a dose of reality, with the cold, hard truth. It hurts. They sometimes don't want to believe it. But when they accept it, they have the chance to turn things around, get back on track, keep progressing towards their goals.

I truly believe that you reach further by standing on the shoulders of giants; find a mentor and you have your giant to climb onto. Oprah's mentor was Maya Angelou. Yves Saint-Laurent's mentor was Christian Dior. Bill Gates's mentor was Warren Buffett. Mark Zuckerberg's mentor was Steve Jobs. My mentors (so far) have been Mark Homer, Andreas Panayiotou and James Caan.

It's not new; it is extremely effective.

I'm a good mentor. I'm not cheap – people pay £50,000 to have me at the end of the phone – but I've got real proof of the results people get when they work with me. I've helped several people become millionaires, I can't count how many people I've helped level up their businesses, achieve really hard goals, and be happier, wealthier and more successful in their lives.

Not all mentors are good, and that's something you have to watch out for. A good mentor will give you what you need when you need it and help you reach your goals. A bad mentor won't have a clue what you need or when you need it. I've seen so many people throw good money after bad on mentors who don't help them at all – and there are a lot of those out there. Here are some tips for staying out of that trap and finding a really good mentor:

1 You get what you pay for; free advice is worth every penny. If you find a good mentor, you'll get a fantastic return on your investment, so as long as it isn't going to put you in danger, be prepared to part with some money.

2 Choose someone who's at least a few steps ahead of you on your journey. Learning to play the piano? Choose someone who's mastered it. Looking to go from five to ten employees? Choose someone who's got 100. Want to make £100 million? Choose a billionaire.

3 Check them out. Do your due diligence before you hand over your cash. Getting an odd feeling? Maybe it's not quite right.

4 Are they a good mentor? Find out from their previous mentees. You can be massively successful in a certain area but dreadful at helping other people get there.

I also help a lot of people get accountability though my social media groups, especially on Facebook. In the Disruptive Entrepreneurs Community, I see people getting public accountability all the time by posting goals, sharing progress, and challenging themselves right there in the group. We've had loads of people do their first Facebook Lives. And now with the Supporter Program, I see it even more.

The Make Cash Challenge I run periodically is a great example of this – at the start of the challenge, people announce their cash goal for the week, then they take daily steps towards that goal. A lot of people are really open about their progress, and they get encouragement and guidance from others in the group. It's a wonderful peer-to-peer mentoring environment.

In the end, you have to figure out what works best for you, what you're able to invest, what your goals are and who can help you reach them.

Summary

Commit to following through with your opportunities – don't let them stagnate, or they'll die right in front of you. Fight procrastination and perfectionism, overwhelm, indecision and fear, and JFDI! Get some accountability to keep you on track – try finding a mentor, or head to a group of supportive people.

TAKE ACTION
. . . .
What are your barriers?

Notice how you're feeling – is there a twinge of perfectionism holding you back? Or a dollop of FOMO? Write down a list of the barriers you're putting up for yourself. Look at it, acknowledge it, then commit to stomping straight over it.

1 Decide on the first logical step. What can you do to get your opportunity moving?
2 What can you commit to doing next?
3 Find at least one person who will hold you accountable for your commitment.
4 Pledge to that person or, if you're really brave, pledge publicly (come on over to my Facebook group – we're good people) what you're going to do.
5 *Just f***ing do it!*

27
Kill your darlings

Like this book, all good things must come to an end.

It's the same for your opportunities. Knowing when and how to kill them is vital if you're going to invite more of them into your life. Sometimes you have to clear the decks.

A while back, a couple of people in my communities mentioned they were getting a bit frustrated by only ever seeing success stories, so I shared a massive list of challenges and failures we've faced over the years. They were great examples of killing your darlings – pulling the plug on an opportunity, whatever stage of growth it's at, especially if you don't want to.

The key is recognizing if you can restart its heart, and accepting when the thing is braindead.

Here are a few of the opportunities we had to kill over the years:

- various different loss-making properties and shitholes
- three bad lettings agencies (one embezzled, one backstabbed and one stole properties)
- staff we pushed too hard (including our own mothers ... how hardcore is that?!).

An opportunity doesn't last for ever. You have to be able to see when it's lights out. Here are some business examples of reasons you might stop an opportunity in motion, and then how to do it:

1 *You're making a financial loss and it's not looking up.* You need to decide (preferably ahead of time) where your line is. If the loss crosses that line, it's time to stop.

2 *You're not interested.* Don't be fickle here – what you're interested in will change over time, but be honest with yourself. If you're no longer interested, then you're probably not invested, so it's not worth your time.

3 *No one else is interested.* This can be a real blind spot. Open your eyes, ask people. If it's a product or a service or a work of art and nobody wants it, maybe it's time to hit pause.

4 *It's too big for you.* Great! You've nailed it! But now it's taking over. Maybe you decide it's best to step away.

There are good ways and bad ways to stop an opportunity when it's rolling. What you don't want to do is burn bridges unnecessarily. Be prepared with an exit strategy that's good for everyone.

1 If you're making a financial loss and it's time to stop, make sure you fulfil your contractual obligations. Repay debts wherever you can.

2 If the opportunity's still 'hot' and it's just not for you any more, find someone who wants to take it on – let them get value from it.

3 If it's not popular and you think it's too early (this happens a lot in the tech world), put it on ice – plan to revisit in three months. If it's just not going to work, bow out gracefully, explain it well to the people involved and thank everyone for their commitment.

4 If it's outgrown you, refer to your exit strategy. If you don't have one, consider selling or getting someone to take over leadership.

When an opportunity dies, it's a chance to embrace change – maybe it helps you grow, maybe it gives you knowledge for your business, maybe it helps you mitigate financial risk in the future. Always look for the upside. Whatever the outcome of the opportunity, it will feed right back into the process of creating the conditions for more to follow.

Are you ready to seize them?

Summary

You need to know how to recognize when it's lights out for an opportunity, and what to do when that time comes. In business, it could be when you're losing money, when no one else is interested or when the thing has grown too big for you to handle. Work hard to end things well, without burning bridges, being graceful and grateful. Whatever the outcome, the lessons will make you even more prepared for the next opportunity.

TAKE ACTION

Choose an opportunity you're working with now. Write an exit strategy.

- What would signal the death of the opportunity?
- How will you decide when to call it a day?
- How will you end it?
- Who would be impacted by the decision?
- Who could take over from you?

Afterword

Our lives are made up of opportunities taken and not taken. Every decision we make shapes what happens next. Here's a timeline of mine, laid bare, so you can see some of the things I've missed and opportunities I've grabbed on my own path.

Opportunities I missed before my 2005 revolution

- I didn't invest in stocks when Dad showed me a news story about a young genius (untouched, my investment would be worth 12 times its original value today).
- I didn't invest in property (house prices in the UK have increased more than 230 percent in the last two decades!).
- I had a successful godfather who I didn't approach for help, advice or support.
- I went to private school, but I never got involved with the rich kids or successful dads – I didn't show enough interest to learn from others and build my network.
- I set up as an artist but never entered enough competitions, never showed my work to enough galleries, never asked clients for any referrals, never tried to get an agent.
- I never really asked for help from anyone who knew more than me – I was too proud, scared and embarrassed.
- I never read books, listened to audio or invested in education and mentors – I assumed you just had to figure it all out yourself and make your own mistakes.

- I always spent money on depreciating liabilities like cars, clothes, electronics and going out drinking, rather than appreciating assets (I had the chance to invest my student loan; instead I spent it on going out, clothes and a video camera).

Opportunities I've taken since 2005

I decided that my life would be very different, and I would TAKE opportunities, instead of letting them pass me by, no matter how scary or how little I knew about them at the time. Here they are in a rough timeline from December 2005 to when I was writing this book.

- I asked my gallery owner friend to recommend property events and opportunities he'd been nagging me for months to get involved in, which opened one door that led to 1,000 more doors...
- I went to my first ever property networking event in December 2005, where I spoke to everyone, handed out my cards, and met my business partner of 15 years... and the boss of a property company gave me my first job.
- I read three books in one week because (my now business partner) Mark Homer recommended them to me, which landed me a job (minimum wage and good commission) at the property company he was working for, with no CV – I took it, despite being scared and inexperienced.
- I learned to sell, which I had always hated; started to listen to sales and personal development programmes (which felt really hard and made me face rejection).
- Selling made me around £100k earnings in 2006, four times as much as I'd ever earned before in a year (imagine if I'd done this in 1999...).

- Working at the property company with Mark led to us buying 20 properties together in our first year and setting up Progressive Property Ltd in January 2007 – a property sourcing company that started our entire business empire of £100m+.
- While this was happening, I was telling my flatmate all about it, who was renting a room from me because, pre-2006, I couldn't afford my full mortgage. When he moved out, he gave me two boxes of CDs – I played them while painting, and it was all spoken word: American, in-your-face and far too happy for my liking. But I kept listening. Those CDs were by Tony Robbins, and this started 15 years of personal development that totally changed my life.
- Through Tony Robbins, I found Chris Howard. My boss paid for me to go to some Chris Howard courses, which led to us getting at least ten £25k fee clients from networking at his events. I did so well from his courses that he used me as a testimonial.
- My boss part paid for me to go to Australia to do Chris' public speaking course, so I could speak at events for my boss and sell his products. He then paid for me to do life coach training, which led to full practice, which led to a mainstream, prime-time TV show on Living TV in 2006 called *Get a Life*.
- This led to me buying my dream house from my hairdresser's Dad (I gave free coaching sessions to my hairdresser).
- These personal development experiences lead me to public speaking for the company, as my boss and Mark didn't want to do it. Public speaking gave me personal confidence I'd always lacked, especially when talking to people I didn't know.

- This led me to talk to a group of women on a night out, one of whom became Mark's wife, and I approached another woman from my gym, who became my wife.
- Public speaking led to me breaking three Guinness World Records for longest speech marathon and raising hundreds of thousands of pounds for various charities.
- Public speaking also led to various contacts, joint ventures and business and has since generated tens of millions of pounds.
- My affinity with Chris Howard gave me a recommendation to buy their promotion partner business, Think Big Education. The company was in trouble; we bought it for £5,000 and turned it around to having an £11m top-line revenue by 2016.
- At that point, we had two big education and events businesses, which led to writing *Property Investing Secrets*, now believed to be the UK's bestselling property how-to guide.
- This has since led to me authoring 18 books, many of which are UK bestsellers.
- The success of *Life Leverage* attracted the world's second biggest publisher to sign me, and this led to 15 translation deals.
- *Property Investing Secrets* and the demand it created led to running our first property training events; this is now a £120m+ revenue business.
- This led to a wealthy client flying us out to the Cayman Islands for private mentoring, which led to us running the Cayman Legacy Mastermind for 10 years and spending one month a year there.
- We then set up one of the top two largest property networks in the UK: Progressive Property Network.
- This led to hosting the year's largest Property Conference in 2010 and meeting James Caan from Dragon's Den...

- Which led to James Caan mentoring us, followed by other multimillionaires and billionaires mentoring us.
- Owning 20 properties with Mark led to raising finance from Mark's mum and stepdad for at least a dozen more deals, and they financed our offices and training suite (we paid them back with interest).
- This de-risked the massive overhead of running events and meant we could scale from two events a year to over 850 training event days a year.
- We had more than 100 properties in three years, then 250 in five years, and this created Progressive Lets – our letting agency, now with almost 1,000 tenants under management.
- The crash of 2008 led to the best, cheapest, highest cash-flowing deals we've probably ever done. (Could COVID present those same opportunities again?)
- Someone whose wife attended one of our courses became a joint venture partner and fully funded a 40-unit conversion project; we still have 50/50 ownership today.
- The promotion/personal development company we bought for £5,000 was awarded Business of the Year in 2016.
- Our property portfolio led to us buying the largest private rental property conversion project in our city (Peterborough).
- Becoming financially free through property led to many (mini) retirements for me, which allowed me to travel the world with my son, who played in the Junior World Golf Championships (under-6) twice in a row. He finished joint second in the UK Championship when he was six, and he had eight holes-in-one by the age of seven.
- Another retirement in 2016 led me to write *Life Leverage* – now at its fifth anniversary and a bestseller.
- It also freed me to launch my *Disruptive Entrepreneur* podcast – now at 10 million downloads and subscribers.

- The podcast has led me to interviewing more than a dozen billionaires and making many famous and successful friends.
- It's also led me to becoming a top Facebook 'influencer' with world top-20 access to Facebook Stars, Facebook Supporters, Facebook Live Events and multiple premium features.
- My podcast led us to building one of the UK's biggest podcast agencies.
- More important than all of this have been the opportunities to meet great people, make great friendships, and to live fully, laugh loudly and love deeply.

Opportunities I've taken since starting to write this book

- I partnered on writing the book *Reinvent Yourself* with Gerald Ratner, which became an instant bestseller.
- I partnered with The Prince's Trust as a RISE board member and launched a 'Young Entrepreneurs Summit'.
- We 'bought' a competitor company with no money down and no fixed overhead.
- We're on the cusp of acquiring more companies to increase our market share.
- I've had many paid keynote gigs on leveraging the lockdown.
- I've had a partnership opportunity with someone who has sold 500 million books.
- We launched a brand new e-commerce Shopify course that has gone wild.

I was recently interviewing the American author Mark Victor Hansen on my *Disruptive Entrepreneur* podcast. We hit it off and became friends, and I told him the story of when I heard him speak. He had said there's no point in having just a few goals, you should have at least 101 goals. So I did what he said and upped my goals to around 200 per year. When I told him I'd done this, he was inspired and asked me to send him some of the goals I'd set and achieved so he could publish them in one of his books! (He's got 312 of them and sold 500 million copies, so I emailed him the next day!)

Here are the goals I sent him, and the details of when I achieved them. Looking back, all of these came from a thought, an intention, and taking an opportunity.

- Learn to fly helicopter (achieved age 29).
- Become a millionaire (achieved age 31).
- Win UK business of the year (achieved in 2016).
- Support my 5-year-old son in sport (he played in the world under-6 golf championships).
- Set up a foundation (I set up the Rob Moore Foundation age 37).
- Raise £1m for charity (we've gone beyond this).
- Buy my dream home (achieved age 35).
- Buy my dream super car – Ferrari Testa Rossa (bought in 2010).
- Have a great podcast (I host the *Disruptive Entrepreneur* podcast, listened to by millions of people around the world).
- Become a bestselling author (achieved with *Money*, *Life Leverage*, *Start Now. Get Perfect Later.* and *I'm Worth More*).
- Host or appear on a major TV show (*Get a Life*, 2006, on Living TV).
- Break a world record (I first broke the world record for the longest public speech marathon in 2013).
- Be a mentor (I now mentor many UK celebrities).
- Get a black belt (I have a brown belt; I'm still working towards the black belt).

- Have a property portfolio (750+ units under management today).
- Have multiple companies and income streams (we now have nine in total).
- Interview the world's most inspiring people (I've interviewed 14 billionaires so far).
- Pay millions in taxes (frequently!).
- Be a great employer and contributor to our local community (we now have 95 staff, hundreds of outsourced workers and over 750 local tenants).
- UK's largest by revenue and community property training company (achieved in 2016).
- Become a global events business (achieved thanks to COVID-19 lockdown).
- Get the best mentor (John DeMartini is now my mentor).
- Random (and non-random) act of kindness or giving every day (I do this now).
- Live. Love. Laugh. (I'm trying every day :-)).
- Be a multi-translated author (I have about 15 translation deals).
- Be an international speaker (I have spoken on stages around the world).

Opportunity is not about how lucky others are, it's about creating your own luck. Opportunity is not about waiting for things to happen, it's about making things happen. Opportunity is not about sitting on your arse, it's about failing forward fast. Start now. Get perfect later. Talk doesn't cook rice. Opportunities are everywhere and infinite.

And remember this: 'if you don't risk anything, you risk everything'.

Bibliography

Other books and media by Rob Moore

I'm Worth More: Realize Your Value. Unleash Your Potential (John Murray Learning, 2019).

Life Leverage: How to Get More Done in Less Time, Outsource Everything & Create Your Ideal Mobile Lifestyle (John Murray Learning, 2016).

Money: Know More, Make More, Give More (John Murray Learning, 2017).

Start Now. Get Perfect Later. (John Murray Learning, 2018).

The Disruptive Entrepreneur, podcast, www.robmoore.com/podcast

www.robmoore.com/

Other books cited in this book

Chopra, D., *The Seven Spiritual Laws of Success: A Practical Guide to the Fulfilment of Your Dreams* (Bantam, 1996).

Eastwood, J. D., Frischen, A., Fenske, M. J., and Smilek, D., 'The unengaged mind', *Perspectives on Psychological Science* 7.5 (2012): 482–95.

Ferriss, T., *The 4-Hour Workweek: Escape the 9–5, Live Anywhere and Join the New Rich* (Vermilion, 2011).

Garcia, G., *The Secret: Law of Attraction: Guide for Absolute Beginners* (CreateSpace, 2015).

Hill, N., *Think and Grow Rich* [1937] (TarcherPerigee, 2016).

Ratner, G., *Gerald Ratner: The Rise and Fall … and Rise Again* (Capstone, 2008).

Ratner, G. and Moore, R., *Reinvent Yourself* (Progressive, 2020).

Wallace, D., *Yes Man* (Ebury Press, 2005).

Wiseman, R., *The Luck Factor: The Scientific Study of the Lucky Mind* (Arrow, 2003).

Other media

Blinkist

Seth Godin, *Akimbo*, podcast

Inside Bill's Brain: Decoding Bill Gates (Netflix, 2019), documentary, directed Davis Guggenheim.

Matt Januszek, *Escape Your Limit*, podcast.

McQueen (2018), film, directed Ian Bonhôte and Peter Ettedgui.

ted.com